Becoming Me

Unraveling and Healing the Sacred Wounds of Religious Trauma in Women

Cassidy DuHadway

Finesse Literary Press Ltd.

First edition 2025 published by Finesse Literary Press Ltd.

Finesse

Contents

Part 3
Becoming Me

Foreword

If this book is in your hands, you're probably carrying something sacred and heavy. Maybe it's your own story. Maybe it's the stories of people you love. Maybe it's the ache of something you haven't quite been able to name until now. I've carried that ache too. It's what led me here. It's what shaped this book.

For years I carried these stories, my own, my clients', and the ones whispered quietly after trainings, in interviews, in small interactions, and in deep conversations with friends and family. Stories of devotion and shame. Of faith and confusion. Of women doing everything right and still feeling like they were the problem. The more I listened, the more I realized that what we were experiencing wasn't just personal pain. It was communal pain. It was generational. It was systemic. And far too often, it was invisible.

This book is not here to challenge your faith or dismantle your belief system. It is not here to tell you whether you should leave or stay or to say that your religious belief is right or wrong. It is here to name the impact of those systems. To hold up a mirror to the unspoken wounds that so many of us carry. The ones we were told to ignore or forgive. The ones that never got words because they were too confusing, too complicated, or too sacred to touch.

It is a book written for women. A voice to counter the voices of men and the systems of men that have spent generations telling us what is and isn't wrong with us without ever stopping to listen. Without ever letting us speak. Without ever offering us space to trust what we already know in our bodies and our souls.

And it is also for those who have experienced similar things. Those who were shaped by the same messages, held to the same impossible standards, or silenced in similar ways. Your story may not look the same, but the ache might feel familiar. Because religious trauma doesn't follow rigid lines. This book is for those who find themselves in the overlap, outside the binaries these systems insist upon but still carrying their wounds.

This book holds story and truth. It weaves together lived experience, clinical understanding, and the quiet wisdom that only comes from years of unlearning. It is part memoir, part map, part invitation to begin again. It is for the woman who left and still feels unsure. The one who stayed but doesn't feel safe. The one who is just beginning to ask if maybe the pain isn't her fault.

You won't find easy answers or quick fixes here. But you will find language. You'll find understanding. You'll find direction. And hopefully, you will start to find yourself.

If you are holding this book, something in you already knows. I hope these pages help you trust it. I hope they help you name what was never yours to carry. I hope they help you begin the work of becoming. Becoming more whole, more honest, more fully your own.

You deserve that.

You always did.

Cassidy DuHadway

Part 1

Unraveling the Sacred Wounds

Finesse Literary Press Ltd.

Chapter 1

The Early Years

Built for Obedience, Taught to Disappear

I was born into a world where the truth was already written. Every answer had a scripture, and every purpose was part of an eternal plan.

I was the oldest child of eight, raised by loving parents who practiced the LDS faith with reverence and devotion. And from the beginning, I wanted to be like them. I wanted to be righteous and good. I wanted to be what they wanted me to be. So I became who my family, the LDS Church, and even Heavenly Father (God) told me to be.

I smiled. I helped. I prayed. I stayed small where I was supposed to and shined just enough to make them proud. I often stood in front of a congregation and bore my testimony or gave a talk. I studied my scriptures and strived to be worthy and righteous, to be like Jesus.

And when something inside me felt off, when the questions got too loud or my feelings didn't fit, I didn't challenge the story.

I challenged myself.

I believed that if I was faithful enough, obedient enough, pure enough, I would be blessed. I would belong. I would find a righteous husband. I would build an eternal family. I would be happy. It was all right there, laid out like a blueprint: be good enough, and it will come.

I remember sitting in Church in Primary, tiny legs swinging off a metal folding chair, doing the hand motions with the rest of the class as we sang about wise men and foolish men, about building on rock and sand.

"The wise man built his house upon the rock,
The wise man built his house upon the rock,
The wise man built his house upon the rock,
And the rains came tumbling down.

The rains came down, and the floods came up,
The rains came down, and the floods came up,
The rains came down, and the floods came up,
And the house on the rock stood still.

The foolish man built his house upon the sand,
The foolish man built his house upon the sand,
The foolish man built his house upon the sand,

And the rains came tumbling down.

The rains came down, and the floods came up,
The rains came down, and the floods came up,
The rains came down, and the floods came up,
And the house on the sand washed away."

As children we sang every word like it was Truth. But as an adult, once I started hearing that song differently, I couldn't un-hear the others. "Follow the Prophet." "I Hope They Call Me on a Mission." "I Am a Child of God." "I Love to See the Temple." "When I Am Baptized." Even "Smiles," "If you chance to meet a frown, do not let it stay. Turn that frown upside down and smile that frown away."

These weren't just songs. They were the foundation. They were emotional choreography. Instructions wrapped in melody, internalized before I ever knew to question them or what they meant. I didn't just believe them. I became them. And I sang them with joy until one day, I didn't.

I believed I was the wise one. I was following the rules. Building on the rock. If I stayed faithful, I would not wash away. But now I know I was building my life on someone else's sand, on their promise of a foundation. It wasn't mine. Not because I was rebellious. Not because I was broken. Not because I wasn't worthy. But because the foundation I was given was never meant to hold me, not my voice, not my doubt, not my strength, not my anger, not my aching need to ask why. Not even my spirituality.

I wasn't building on rock. I was performing on a stage. I didn't have a foundation. I had a script. And when the rains came, when life cracked open, when the promises stopped working, when I could no longer pretend, the house didn't stand firm. It collapsed. And I collapsed with it.

That collapse. . . that quiet, invisible, devastating unraveling. . . that's where the story of religious trauma begins.

This book is for anyone who knows that kind of unraveling. It's for the ones who built everything exactly the way they were told and still watched it fall apart. For the ones who tried to be good, righteous, obedient, and virtuous. For the ones who gave everything to a version of faith that never made space for their full humanity.

This book is a conversation, not a lecture. It is here to name things that maybe you have not been able to name. It is here to help you feel less alone.

This book speaks specifically from within the experience of the LDS Church (The Church of Jesus Christ of Latter-day Saints). While many of the patterns of religious trauma are recognizable across different systems, the stories and teachings I draw from are rooted in the world of LDS culture and doctrine. This is the lens I know best. It is the system that shaped me, and it is the system I am writing from and writing to. If you come from another faith background, you may still find echoes here because many religious traditions share similar dynamics. The details may differ, but the emotional imprint often feels familiar. I hope you see your story reflected in these pages, even if the language or context is not exactly the same as your own.

I wrote it for two groups of people. First, for those who are untangling their own experiences, especially women and others who were taught to stay small, quiet, or selfless in the name of faith. If that's you, I want you to know that what happened matters. If that is you, I want you to know that what happened matters. What you experienced is valid. You are not too sensitive. You are not making it up. You do not have to throw away everything you believed, but you also do not have to keep pretending that nothing hurts. Whether you still believe, do not believe, or are not sure anymore, you deserve to feel whole.

Second, I wrote it for the professionals, the therapists, leaders, and helpers who want to do better. Who want to understand the kind of harm that does not leave bruises but still leaves people in pieces. Who are ready to meet others with empathy instead of advice. Who are willing to listen to the voices that have been dismissed for far too long.

This is not a book about doctrine. It is a book about people. It's about their stories. Their Pain. Their Healing. It's about Hope.

And it starts here, with the moment you stop doubting what you have always known deep down and start listening to the quiet truth that has been with you all along. That truth has a name. And in the next chapter, we will begin calling it what it is.

Chapter 2

Foundations of Religious Trauma

How We Were Conditioned

When I was a child, I was given a ring. A simple green shield with three letters stamped into the silver: CTR. Choose the Right. I wore it every day, twisting it around my finger like a spell. It wasn't just jewelry. It was a promise. A warning. A command.

I was told that if I followed the rules, everything would fall into place. That obedience would bring peace and prosperity. That righteousness would bring eternal love and belonging. So I followed the rules. I studied the scriptures. I went to every activity. I tried to be gentle and patient. I smiled when I didn't feel like smiling. I quieted the parts of me that didn't belong, parts that were too loud, too sensitive, or simply too different.

But belonging never came. My worth wasn't inherent. No matter how perfectly I played the part, I never felt like I truly fit. Like something about me was always just slightly off. Either too much or not enough.

I didn't understand what was wrong. I just knew that being fully myself wasn't allowed. That emotions were messy, inappropriate, and best kept hidden. That expressing them or having needs made me selfish, or worse, bad. So I learned how to disappear. I learned to carry it all quietly. To hold my own pain and make space for everyone else's. Their comfort. Their feelings. Their spiritual safety.

And underneath it all was a truth I never spoke out loud: Love had to be earned. Worth had to be proven. Belonging had to be bought in silence and sacrifice.

I was told that God's love was unconditional. But I was also taught that I had to earn it. By being obedient. By following the plan. By holding tight to the rod. Maybe they didn't mean to make it feel conditional. Maybe they truly believed love was constant. But the message underneath it, the message I received was different: God's love could be lost. And if I wanted to keep it, I had to prove I was worthy of it. Over and over again.

I didn't know this was trauma. No one around me used that word. But my body knew. It learned to shut down. I learned how to perform, pretending that everything was 'FINE' instead of being able to feel when things weren't. And when the ache of never being enough grew too strong, it learned to numb that pain. Long before I had language for it, my nervous system had already adapted to survive.

At the time, I believed I was the problem. It took years of healing and holding the stories of others before I could see what was really happening. These patterns weren't just mine. I began to see them in the quiet moments people shared with me, in the tension they carried, the shame they couldn't name, and the way they blamed themselves for not being good enough or worthy.

This is more than a personal story. It is a pattern. It shows up in homes, churches, relationships, and systems where love is promised but comes with conditions. Where safety is spoken of but rarely felt. Where the cost of staying is the slow disappearance of your voice and your needs. And the price of belonging is conformity. Sacrificing parts of yourself in order to stay.

What comes next is not a list of definitions or a clinical breakdown. It is a gentle unpacking of what trauma really is and how it works in the head, heart, and body. Not all at once and not to convince you of anything. Just one layer at a time.

When Safety Breaks

Trauma isn't just what happens to us. It's what happens inside us.

> "Trauma is not simply an event that happened in the past; it is a wound that stays with you in the present. It is the imprint of pain, horror, and fear living on inside the person."
>
> Judith Herman, Trauma and Recovery

When most people hear the word trauma, they picture something extreme: a car accident, a violent attack, a life-threatening moment. And yes, those are real and devastating forms of trauma.

But not all trauma is big and loud. Some trauma is quiet and consistent. It happens slowly in relationships and environments where safety should exist but doesn't. It's not always about what happened. Sometimes it's about what never happened or the comfort that never came. The presence that was never offered. The parts of you that were never welcomed or made room for.

These are the wounds of emotional neglect, chronic shame, and conditional love. They don't scream. They whisper.

> *Be nice. Be sweet. Be gentle. Be a light. Be reverent. Be a good helper. Don't ask questions. Choose the right, even when no one is watching, even when it hurts. Don't cry too much. Don't be dramatic. Smile. Cover up; you don't want to distract the boys. Don't make anyone uncomfortable. Be the kind of girl a righteous man would choose. Be virtuous. Be patient. Be the kind of girl who makes her parents proud. Be righteous. Be worthy. Be the kind of woman God can trust.*

And over time, those whispers shape everything.

Trauma isn't defined by the size of the event. It's defined by how your nervous system experiences it. If you felt unsafe, unworthy, unloved, unseen, unheard, trapped, abandoned, or like you didn't matter, even for a moment, that's a wound. And when those wounds aren't seen, named, or healed, they don't just disappear. They become trauma. Especially when it happens again and again.

This is what we call complex trauma. The kind that's woven into your development. The kind that doesn't come from one moment but from a thousand small wounds. It's chronic, relational, identity-based. It changes the way you see yourself, the way you relate to others, the way you move through the world.

And for many of us, especially those raised in rigid or deeply religious environments, this is where the trauma lives. Not in violence. But in the quiet expectations to be what you aren't. The impact of this trauma is much more subtle. It comes, in T.S. Eliot's words, 'not with a bang but with a whimper' in the quiet disappearance of self.

Anna's Story

Her name was Anna.

She couldn't understand why she felt exhausted all the time. She took care of everyone. Her partner. Her kids. Her parents. Her church. Her ward. She was the one people relied on, the one who always had it together. But inside, she felt hollow.

We traced that exhaustion back to something early. When Anna was young, her mom was rushing to get dinner on the table before her dad got home from work. The baby was crying. The toddler had spilled a

15

bowl of cereal. And Anna stood nearby holding a book, asking, "Will you read this to me?"

Her mom didn't scold her. She didn't raise her voice. She just gave her a tired smile and said, "Sweetheart, can you be my big helper instead? I really need you right now."

And so she did. She set the book down. Wiped up the milk. Picked up the spoon. Bounced the baby while her mom stirred the sauce. She didn't cry. She didn't ask again. She was the good girl.

No one called it trauma. But something in her body shifted that day.

A belief took root: Being good means taking care of others. Wanting connection makes things harder. If I stay quiet and helpful, I'll be loved.

She was four.

And like so many women I know, Anna didn't just carry the baby. She carried the belief. That being good meant taking care of others. That wanting connection only made things harder. That if she stayed quiet and helpful, she'd be loved. She was four.

So many women I've worked with have stories like this. Not loud or dramatic. Just a thousand small moments that felt normal at the time. Moments that seemed like nothing but left wounds. Tiny ones that were never named, never tended to, never healed. Their bodies remember. The tightening in their chest when they ask for help. The guilt that creeps in when they rest. The ache they can't explain when no one notices their pain. The panic that rises just from thinking about saying no.

If you find yourself always helping, always holding, always carrying more than your share, maybe it started early. Maybe there was a moment when your need was met with pressure. When being "good" meant staying quiet. When connection started to feel like something you had to earn. You don't have to remember the exact moment. Your nervous system already does.

And maybe now you're wondering how something so small could go so deep. That's where we start next: with how trauma actually works. How it's not about what happened on the outside but what was felt deeply on the inside.

Trauma Is Subjective and Developmental

Trauma is subjective and developmental. It is deeply personal.

Two people can live through the same moment; one walks away relatively fine, and the other carries a wound for decades. It's not because one is weaker. It's because trauma isn't about what happened. It's about how your system perceived the situation, whether it registered safety or threat.

And that perception of safety or threat is deeply shaped by your stage of development.

A four year-old doesn't have the language or context to understand why a parent is distant or emotionally unavailable. They don't think,

"Mom is overwhelmed," or "Dad is preoccupied." They think, "I must have done something wrong."

At that age, survival depends on connection. So even subtle moments of disconnection, being ignored, brushed off, or told to "be a good girl" when they're upset can register as a threat. Not because the moment was dramatic but because the child's sense of self and safety is still forming.

As children grow, the same system keeps scanning. But now, it's not just about attachment. It's identity, belonging, and social safety.

A twelve-year-old who asks a sincere question in Sunday School about gender roles or eternal families and gets shut down with a forced smile and a scripture verse might not experience physical danger. But their body still registers the silence, the subtle disapproval, the shift in the room. They feel it in their chest. In their throat. In their stomach.

And without context, their nervous system assigns meaning: I'm not safe when I speak. My questions make people pull away. I need to be quiet to stay accepted.

Again, it's not always about what happened. It's about how the system learned to adapt to stay safe.

The Body Remembers First

We don't just think our way through life. We sense our way through it.

Our bodies are constantly scanning for cues: Am I safe? Am I wanted? Do I belong here?

This scanning is done through the nervous system, a beautiful, automatic part of us that is always working to protect us. You don't have to instruct it. It senses. It responds. It remembers. And it predicts.

> *If you are reading this as a therapist, know that your client may not have words for this yet. Trauma often lives in the body before it finds language. The work is in trusting the story the body already knows.*

It's the part of you that pulls back before you even know why. The part that tenses when someone walks into the room. The part that goes quiet when the energy shifts.

When we experience trauma, especially when it's ongoing, subtle, or relational, the nervous system doesn't just react in the moment. It learns. And then it begins to anticipate. It uses everything it has seen, heard, and felt to prepare for what might come next. Not because something is wrong with you. But because that's what safety looks like in a body that has had to adapt.

So when something familiar stirs in you. Like a voice, a look, a silence, a thought, a belief, a smell, or a sensation. Your nervous system does not pause to double-check. It responds. It moves. It protects.

And when that kind of response becomes a repeated experience, your body starts seeing the world through that lens. Just in case. Because it would rather overprotect than be underprepared.

This is not weakness. This is the beauty and the pain of survival.

What Is Religious Trauma?

Religious trauma is what happens when the religious or spiritual system that promised to love you, guide you, and keep you safe becomes a source of harm, shame, and disconnection. It's not always about a dramatic event. Sometimes it's about the air you breathe, the messages you absorb so early they shape how you see yourself, how you move through the world, and what you believe you're allowed to feel.

In the context of the Church of Jesus Christ of Latter Day Saints, these messages often come in familiar phrases. You're told, "Your body is a temple." It's sacred, holy. But then you're also told it's dangerous. That it can lead boys astray. That you must cover it up, hide it, and manage it because a righteous woman wouldn't distract anyone. You learn to feel ashamed of the very thing you were told is divine.

You're told, "You are responsible for the spiritual well-being of others." Women are taught to be the gatekeepers of morality, responsible for the purity of relationships, the emotions of others, the success of their families, and the faith of their children. If something goes wrong, it must be because you didn't pray enough, weren't faithful enough, or weren't quiet or submissive enough.

You hear, "Don't be angry." Girls are taught to be sweet, gentle, and forgiving. Anger is seen as unrighteous, something to repent of. You can feel sad or overwhelmed, but only in ways that are soft, quiet, and palatable. And boys? They're not allowed to be soft at all. No tears, no tenderness, no vulnerability. They're expected to be strong, in control, and emotionally sealed off unless they're bearing their testimony.

You're taught to "follow the prophet," even if what he says doesn't sit right. Even if it contradicts your inner knowing. Even if it causes harm. Because obedience is elevated above understanding, and questioning is treated as a threat to faith.

You're told to "doubt your doubts." When you voice concerns, you're met with pity, scripture, or silence. You're told to push it down, keep praying, and try harder. And when the answers don't come, you assume the problem is you.

And then there are "eternal families." You're told it's the greatest gift. Forever love. The ultimate reward. But for some, it becomes a prison. A promise used to keep you tethered to people or roles that no longer fit or that actively harm you. Like the woman who stays with an unsupportive or abusive husband, not because it feels safe or right but because she believes leaving might risk her eternal wellbeing and that of her children. When you're raised inside that story, leaving doesn't just mean walking away. It means destroying everything.

Religious trauma often includes chronic shame around your body, thoughts, desires, or doubts. It involves emotional suppression, especially of anger, grief, or longing. It is grounded in conditional love and belonging, tied to righteousness or obedience. It often uses spiritual bypassing, where faith is used to avoid real pain. It reinforces fear-based control through teachings on eternal consequences. And it includes gendered expectations, where women carry the emotional and spiritual weight of everyone else, and men are stripped of their softness.

And for many, this includes the interruption of typical childhood, adolescence, and sexual development. Curiosity, desire, and autonomy are treated as threats rather than natural parts of becoming. Sexuality is delayed, distorted, or shamed into silence. Even after marriage, confusion, pain, or numbness around sex often persist long after the rules are gone.

When all of this is delivered in the name of love, whether from leaders, family, scripture, or a God you were taught to trust unconditionally, it becomes almost impossible to see clearly. Because those beliefs aren't just ideas. They are tied to the people who raised you, to the relationships that shaped you, to your sense of being good, loved, and worthy. They are tangled into your spirituality, identity, and understanding of who you're supposed to be. So whether you're beginning to question, trying to stay, or still fully devout, the pain lives in the tension. You are not just wrestling with doctrine. You are not just wrestling with doctrine. You are wrestling with love, loyalty, and worthiness. With who you are, and who you're not allowed to be.

This is religious trauma. It deserves to be named. Because it doesn't just shape what you believe. It shapes who you become.

Spiritual Bypassing

Spiritual bypassing is using spirituality to avoid, dismiss, or silence real emotional pain. It asks people to perform healing before they are ready, instead of honoring the messy, necessary work of feeling and processing.

Examples -
"Everything Happens for a Reason"
"You have to Forgive"
"You'll be grateful for this one day"
"Maybe you're struggling cuz you're not faithful enough."
"Patience is a Virtue"

What to Do Instead:
Validate the pain before offering meaning.
Sit with the discomfort instead of rushing past it.
Say, "It makes sense that this hurts."
Honor that healing takes time, and it's okay to not feel okay.
Support people in telling the truth about their experience, even if it's messy, angry, or unresolved.

When God Becomes the Attachment Figure

Religious trauma is complex trauma. Like all complex trauma, it often begins at the intersection of development and attachment. These are the early, formative years when we learn what love feels like, what safety requires, and what parts of us are welcome. In some religious systems, especially those that emphasize obedience, righteousness, and eternal outcomes, those early attachment lessons are shaped not only by caregivers but by spiritual expectations. You're taught that blessings come through obedience. That worth is tied to performance. That belonging depends on staying faithful, good, and quiet.And you're taught to feel it. The presence of the Holy Ghost was held up as confirmation, a spiritual witness that you were doing it right. Peace, clarity, or warmth meant you were on the right path. Silence, fear, or confusion meant you had gone astray. So even your emotions became a measure of righteousness.

For many of us, God was introduced as an attachment figure. Not just a divine being but someone who loved us perfectly, guided our choices, and knew us better than we knew ourselves. We were taught to trust Him more than our own instincts. To hand over our decisions, our desires, and even our inner voice because He knew what was best. And because He was perfect, the relationship itself became unquestionable. If we felt distant from Him, if the guidance stopped coming, if our prayers went unanswered, the problem couldn't be with Him. It had to be with us. We must have sinned. We must not have enough faith. We must not be worthy. So we didn't question the system. We questioned ourselves.

And woven into all of it was the Holy Ghost, the still, small voice that was supposed to confirm the truth, offer comfort, and warn us when we were on the wrong path. We were taught to feel Him. Peace, warmth, or clarity meant we were in alignment. Confusion, fear, or silence meant we had strayed. Our emotional states became spiritual feedback. Even our nervous systems became evidence of our righteousness or failure.

Religious trauma often begins with the quiet, invisible shaping of your inner world. When love, safety, and connection are tied to how well you conform, attachment itself becomes conditional. From your earliest years, you learn to suppress your needs, minimize your emotions, and perform for approval because love, worth, and belonging depend on staying aligned with the system. This kind of environment doesn't just shape you; it stalls your natural development. Emotional, moral, and even relational growth often gets frozen at the point where obedience took priority over exploration or autonomy.

The more demanding, controlling, and fundamental your religious experience was, the more likely this became your foundation. Not just in what you believed but in how you saw yourself. In how you formed relationships. In how you learned to survive. It arrested your childhood and teenage development. Not in a dramatic or obvious way but in the quiet, ongoing ways that taught you to disconnect from yourself in order to belong. It didn't just shape your faith. It shaped your nervous system. It became your internal belief system.

Religious Abuse

Religious abuse occurs when spiritual authority is used to manipulate, control, exploit, or harm. It goes beyond pressure or expectation and becomes coercion. It turns guidance into domination, influence into violation. And while some forms of religious abuse are overt and recognizable, loud, forceful, and even violent, others are subtle, polite, and cloaked in the language of righteousness.

That's what makes it so disorienting. Religious abuse often comes wrapped in scripture, embedded in callings, spoken from the pulpit, or delivered by people who say they love you. It's not always what's done in secret; it's often what's normalized in plain sight.

Religious abuse can take many forms. It includes spiritual manipulation, like using scripture or doctrine to control behavior, silence dissent, or justify harm. It includes sexual abuse or grooming, especially when power dynamics are spiritualized or hidden behind ideas like callings, worthiness, or divine authority. Emotional abuse is also common. It often takes the form of belittling, shaming, or gaslighting someone in the name of obedience, faith, or eternal salvation. There's social control, too, where threats to someone's belonging, community, or afterlife are used to force compliance. Gender-based domination is often justified through religious roles, using priesthood authority or doctrine to reinforce male control and female submission. And religious abuse thrives in environments that protect the institution above all else, where secrecy and silence are demanded to avoid "hurting the Church" or making others uncomfortable.

It's also important to name that physical abuse and sexual assault are sometimes carried out in the name of God. These are not just violations of the body; they are violations of trust, spirit, and safety. When a person in spiritual authority hits, touches, or coerces another human being and justifies it as divine will, discipline, or sacred intimacy, the wound goes even deeper. Survivors are left questioning not just what happened but whether God approved of it. That kind of confusion is devastating. It hijacks the nervous system, erodes self-trust, and leaves a survivor holding unbearable questions: Was it my fault? Did I sin? Am I still worthy? Was God watching, and did He turn away?

And for those who spoke up, who did the brave and terrifying thing and told someone. They often encountered a second layer of trauma. Many turned to their family, bishop, stake president, or other spiritual leaders, believing they would be protected. Instead, they were told to forgive. To keep quiet. To avoid disrupting the peace of the community. Often, the abuser was shielded, defended, or moved to a new position of authority while the survivor was left to carry the consequences. This is a sacred betrayal, when the very system meant to offer safety and healing becomes a tool of silencing and harm.

What makes religious abuse especially painful is how often it is sanctified. In systems where authority is unquestionable and obedience is seen as holiness, abuse can look like faithfulness. Victims are taught to stay quiet, be forgiving, and carry their pain alone. They're told it's a trial, a refining fire, a test of faith. They're praised for their endurance, loyalty, and ability to suffer well. And all the while, they're left holding the cost.

Being abused or harmed by someone in spiritual power doesn't mean you lack faith. It doesn't make you weak. It means the system failed you. If your body still tenses in church buildings, if your stomach turns at the sound of a hymn, if the mention of God makes your heart race, it may not be just discomfort. It may be your body remembering something it was never allowed to name.

Religious trauma and abuse aren't always visible, and they aren't always intentional. But the effects are real. They distort your relationship with spirituality, trust, and love. And they deserve to be seen for what they are.

If This Feels Familiar

Religious trauma is real. It's valid. It's layered, often invisible, and deeply embedded in the stories we were given about love, safety, and who we're allowed to be. For many of us, it shaped us before we had the chance to grow into ourselves, emotionally, relationally, even sexually.

As you read through these definitions and examples, you may have felt something stirred by recognition, resistance, confusion, or maybe even grief. Parts of this chapter might have felt too close. Maybe others didn't fit at all. That's okay. You get to decide how your experience is named, whether you consider it religious trauma, religious abuse, both, or something else entirely. Your story is yours to hold and yours to honor.

As we move forward, I'll be using the term *religious trauma* to describe the experiences I've lived through, witnessed, and supported others in healing. This term holds a wide range of experiences, including abuse, neglect, complex trauma, and spiritual harm. All trauma that happens within religious or spiritual contexts, whether those experiences were purposeful or unintentional. It's the language that allows me to speak to the full impact of those experiences while doing my best to help your system stay grounded and not overactivated (if I have any say in that at all). But please know, you're never required to adopt the same words. Use whatever language feels true for you. You are allowed to engage with this book in a way that honors your pace, your process, and your nervous system. You're welcome here, exactly where you are.

Trauma does not need to be catastrophic to be real. It does not need to be physical to leave bruises. Religious trauma can live deep inside our attachment systems, nervous systems, bodies, and sense of self, long before we ever have the words to name it.

Naming it now is not about blaming the past. It is about breaking the silence inside you.

You were not weak for needing safety. You were not wrong for needing to be seen.

You may still be unsure if what you experienced "counts." You might be questioning whether your pain is valid or wondering if you're just being dramatic. That's normal. Most of us were never given the language to name this kind of harm, especially when it came wrapped in righteousness.

But if something in you has stirred as you've read, if your body tensed or your chest sank or something deep inside whispered, *this is me*, then please hear this: You are not making it up. You are not alone.

You're allowed to look at the foundation you were given. You're allowed to name the cracks.

Now that we've named the foundation, I want to share how it looked in my life.

The next chapter is my story, not because it's the only one or the most important one but because it's the path I know best. It's where the words I've written so far became real. And where my healing began.

Reflection:

When did you first learn that being good, obedient, or faithful mattered more than being you?

Gentle Practice:

Place your hand over your heart. Breathe in. Breathe out. Take a moment and give yourself permission to allow your story exactly as it is. You are not asking too much. You are remembering what was always yours.

Chapter 3

When God Broke My Heart

The Beginning of the Undoing

I didn't know it then, but this was the moment everything would change. It was the moment God betrayed me.

Music has always been part of my life. Like many Mormon (LDS) girls, I was taught piano when I was young. I don't remember how much I practiced or played, but I do remember arguing with my mom about having to practice when I didn't want to. Somewhere along the way, something began to settle in. Music started to matter.

In seventh grade, I joined the school band, and that's when everything started to shift. I fell in love with music, with playing, with performing, with practicing. Music became mine. I became a drummer, a percussionist. It gave me a place to belong. It gave me friends, a way to express myself, and teachers who saw me. For the first time, I had something that was just mine.

I loved it. And I was good at it.

By the time I reached college, I knew I wanted to keep playing. Music wasn't just something I did. It was where I felt most alive. The rhythm, the movement, the feeling of being part of something bigger than myself. It felt like connection. Like purpose. But it wasn't the kind of purpose I had been taught to aim for. I was a drummer. I hit stuff with sticks. And it was awesome.

Still, it didn't fit the plan I was raised with. It wasn't soft piano music for Sunday services. It wasn't meant to accompany a choir or prepare me for a future in Relief Society. It was bold. It took up space. And it didn't point directly to temple marriage or motherhood. I had to fight to study music. Fight to be taken seriously. Fight to stay on a path that didn't look like the covenant one I had been taught to follow. But I got in. And once I did, I didn't stop.

I spent my whole college career in it. Four years of waking up before sunrise to get time in the practice rooms. Four years of staying up late, perfecting every detail. I played in the orchestra, the jazz band, small ensembles, with the choir, in the symphonic band, and in the pit for musicals. I performed professionally with small groups and with the Utah Opera Company. My senior year, I gave an entire solo concert as my capstone project. I was also selected as a concerto soloist, performing marimba with the symphony orchestra.

It wasn't just about talent. It was work. Discipline. Hours and hours of devotion. And I loved it.

Music wasn't just something I did. It was who I was.

At church, I was often called to be the pianist in Relief Society, at events, and in sacrament meetings. At one point, I was even asked to play the organ. I had never played before, but I said yes anyway. I was taught to say yes to callings. No wasn't even an answer I knew I could give. Week by week, my ward experienced the process of learning how to play the organ during sacrament right along with me. I can still cringe at all the wrong notes I played in every carefully crafted hymn. But it felt like part of how I served. Part of how I worshipped. Music was part of my connection to the divine.

So when I say this moment changed everything, I don't say that lightly.

I was about to graduate from college with my music performance degree. I'd spent years pouring everything into my music. I loved it. It was all I wanted to do.

I was a percussionist, a marimba player, and I was good. I'd wake up early every day to practice, pouring hours into perfecting my craft. My dream was clear: I was going to go to graduate school and study music so I could perform professionally as a concert percussionist. I was going to perform in recording rooms and be in professional orchestras. I was going to stand on stages and play music, I was going to teach others how to play. It was my spiritual gift. My way to bear testimony without words.

But music wasn't the only thing shaping my life. I had always been deeply committed to my faith. I attended church every Sunday without fail, served in my callings, and made daily scripture study and prayer a priority. My life was carefully structured around obedience to God, and I believed wholeheartedly that if I followed Him, He would guide me to where I was supposed to be.

At the same time, I was working toward what I believed was the "right" dream and plan: to get married and have children. That expectation was woven into everything I did, and I had been trying to make it happen. But it hadn't happened yet. As I neared graduation, I didn't have a family, and I felt the weight of that deeply. With that part of my life still uncertain, I believed it made sense to pour myself into my passion for music, a path that felt right and fulfilling.

So I prayed, again and again. Every night, I knelt down and begged Heavenly Father for guidance. *Please tell me this is where I'm meant to go. Please tell me this is the right choice. Since your plan for me, the marriage and family I've been working toward, hasn't happened yet, this is what I'll do until then. This is my dream. Please let me know if it's right.* I trusted Him to provide the answers I needed because that's what I had always been taught: if you ask in faith, God will answer.

I never received a solid answer. So I started moving toward grad school. I started applying to my top universities and was dreaming about who I would be studying with. During my last year of school, I got to go to PASIC, an international percussion convention in Columbus, Ohio. It was incredible. I saw all the greats, met so many amazing musicians, and felt so excited about my future.

But I still hadn't received a firm answer. My excitement, decision, and commitment weren't enough. I had to have the stamp of approval from Heavenly Father. So I found a quiet hallway, surrounded by the hum of drums and the energy of percussionists from all over the world, and I prayed one more time. With my full faith in God, and with everything in me, I asked.

And then, I got an answer.

No.

And in that moment, I felt the world drop out from under me. My knees buckled, and I sank down against the wall. My stomach was in knots, tears streaming silently down my face. I was devastated. People passed by, oblivious, as I sat there crying. I was surrounded by so many people, but I had never felt so utterly alone.

It didn't feel just like a no. It felt like a command to abandon everything I loved. A requirement. A divine expectation. A quiet withdrawal of permission.

> *'You need to be home with your children. You need to be a mother. A wife. A musician's life will never work. You won't be a good mom if you do that. I want you to stay home. That's where you're supposed to be.'*

That moment didn't just break my heart. It broke my whole world. I didn't see it for what it was because I had wrapped my whole self around the belief that God loved me. That if I was faithful enough, obedient enough, God would never ask me to give up something so sacred. I was betrayed.

I believed the answer. I trusted in the Holy Ghost. I believed it was God's will.

But a huge part of me wanted to scream.

> *'Why would God ask me to bury my talent? Why would He take away the very thing He had given me? He knew me. He knew how much I loved it. He knew this dream lived in me. Why would He bless me with a gift, help me grow it, let me love it, and then tell me I couldn't magnify it?'*

The doubt didn't go away. It stayed, tucked deep inside the hollow I was already carrying. It felt dangerous. Scary. And I didn't know what to do with it.

So I chose Heavenly Father. I chose eternal salvation. I chose to ignore my struggle and lean into obedience. Faith was everything.

I didn't have the language for it at the time, but now I do. When I asked God for permission to follow the path that made me come alive, and He said no, that answer didn't come out of nowhere. It came from the parts of me that had already learned how to abandon myself.

Religious trauma isn't always loud. Sometimes it's quiet. Sometimes it sounds like obedience. Like humility. Like letting go. I had been conditioned, over and over, to believe that when something didn't fit, the problem was me. My wants. My desires. My dreams.

So when I asked if I could be different, if I could stay with something that made me feel whole, that I was passionate about, I didn't just hear no. I heard exactly what the system had trained me to hear. 'No' wasn't just the Holy Ghost. It wasn't just God's voice. It was the voice of all the small moments that taught me to give myself up in the name of being righteous.

And because I had been taught to obey Him above all else, I did what He told me to do: I walked away. I put my drumsticks down that day, and I didn't play percussion or marimba again for over twelve years. It wasn't the first time I let go of a part of myself, and it wouldn't be the last. I gave up parts of myself in the name of obedience. I just didn't know that yet.

I gave up my dream, not because I wanted to but because I believed it was what God asked of me.

I had done everything I was supposed to do. I practiced. I performed. I worked hard. I was disciplined. And I was doing all the spiritual things too: scripture study, prayer, temple worship, callings. I was trying so hard to be righteous. To be faithful. To be worthy. I believed that righteous women sacrificed what they loved. I believed that wanting too much made me selfish. I believed that following God's will mattered more than anything I wanted. I believed that if I gave everything to God, my time, my talent, my heart, I would be blessed.

I had poured myself into becoming the kind of person I was taught to be. Spiritually. Musically. I thought it would be enough. But it wasn't. Not for God. Not for the life I had been promised. And everything I had built my worth around started to fall apart.

Obeying God's answer to walk away from music was supposed to bring me peace. That's what I had been taught my whole life: when you follow His will, you'll feel His love and comfort.

But I didn't feel peace. I felt hollow and lost.

Walking away from music wasn't just about giving up a dream. It felt like I was giving up a part of myself. I had spent years pouring my heart into this craft, shaping my identity, dreaming of my future around the music I loved. And now, it was gone. My days were quieter. Emptier. I avoided my instruments entirely; I couldn't even look at the marimba without feeling the ache of what I had lost.

It wasn't just the music. It was who I got to be when I played. It was the one place where everything inside me felt like it belonged.

Music was one of the only places I was allowed to be fully myself. Where I didn't have to shrink to be acceptable. It was where I felt most like myself, connected to something deeper. It was also how I felt the Spirit. Not just in quiet prayers or soft Sunday hymns but in rhythm. In sound. In the way music moved through me. It was worship. It was sacred.

When I gave it up, I didn't just lose a dream. I lost the part of me that knew how to breathe. I lost one of the few places I felt connected to God.

And then came the hardest part: telling the people who had trained me, supported me, and believed in me that I wasn't going to grad school. I had worked so hard to earn their trust and respect. My professors, mentors, and fellow musicians had seen my potential, invested in me, and celebrated my accomplishments. And now I had to face them, knowing I was about to let them down.

I remember the hollow, sinking feeling in my chest every time I had to say the words out loud: *I'm not going.* It felt like I was betraying everyone around me. They had poured so much into me, and now, I was walking away from everything we'd worked toward. There was no way to explain my decision that didn't feel small or inadequate. I couldn't say *God told me not to* without seeing the confusion, or worse, the disappointment on their faces.

The worst part was that I couldn't even tell them how much it hurt. How much I wanted to stay. How much I wanted to go to grad school and keep chasing the dream we had all believed in. Instead, I offered half-smiles and vague explanations, pretending I was okay while I felt like I was breaking apart inside.

After each conversation, I walked away feeling more alone than before. It wasn't just the loss of music. It was the growing distance from the people who had been part of that world. I didn't belong there anymore. I didn't belong anywhere. I was drifting farther and farther away from everything that had once anchored me.

I graduated that year with zero plans. All my friends were getting married, going to music school, or starting their lives with perfect families and relationships headed toward temple marriages. I was supposed to be one of them. I was supposed to have a path. Instead, I felt like I had been dropped into a void. I had obeyed. I had done everything right. And now I was standing in the silence, completely alone. No plan. No future. No dream left to chase. Just the ache of everything I'd lost.

I didn't know where to go, so I ran. I threw myself into something completely different, something hard and physical and brutal enough to keep me from thinking. I became a wildland firefighter, putting my body on the line every day, trying to prove I could still matter. Trying to find something, *anything*, that could fill the space music used to hold.

At the time, I thought the pain of walking away from music was the hardest part of obeying God's will. It felt like everything had shattered in that moment. But what I didn't understand yet was that the cracks had been there all along. That moment didn't just break my heart. It started to expose the fractures in the foundation I had built my life on. A foundation that belonged to someone else that was shaped by obedience, silence, and cutting off parts of myself. I had been living inside that system for years. I just hadn't seen it until my world shattered around me.

Suppressing Emotions and Silencing Doubts

For as long as I can remember, I was taught that feelings weren't just unreliable; they were right or wrong. Good feelings, I learned, came from God. They were a sign I was on the right path, doing the right things, and being faithful. Bad feelings like anger, sadness, and frustration, however, came from Satan. They were a warning that something was wrong, not with the situation but with me. If I was upset, doubtful, or uncomfortable, it wasn't because something needed to change. It was because I needed to repent, pray harder, or realign myself with God's will.

This belief shaped how I related to my emotions from a very young age. By the time I was three, I had already started to distrust myself and my experiences. If I felt hurt or confused, I didn't question the situation. I questioned myself. I internalized the idea that emotions weren't to be listened to. They were to be corrected. And so, I learned to suppress.

When I look back now, I can see how deeply this suppression impacted me. As I grew older, I silenced the little voice inside me that said, *This doesn't feel right.* Sometimes that discomfort would land in my body, a tight chest, a sick stomach, a heaviness I couldn't name. But I learned to ignore it. I called it weakness. I called it temptation. I didn't yet know it was my body trying to protect me.

I dismissed the discomfort I felt when I struggled to align my dreams and desires with the expectations laid out for me. When my heart whispered questions, I buried them beneath prayers and scriptures. Faith, I believed, meant ignoring my feelings and trusting God instead.

At the time, I didn't recognize what I was doing as suppression. It felt like faithfulness. When I was upset or overwhelmed, I told myself to push those feelings aside and pray harder. *You just need to be more*

41

faithful, I would think. *If you're struggling, it's because you're not doing enough.*

Walking away from music was one of the clearest examples of this pattern. I remember how heartbroken I felt, how deeply I wanted to cry out to God, *Why would You ask this of me? Why would You take this away?* A part of me wanted to yell, to rage, to demand answers. *How could this be love? How could this be right?* But I didn't let myself go there. I was terrified of what it would mean if God could be wrong, or worse, if I couldn't trust what I thought was His voice. So I shut it down. I told myself to be grateful for His guidance, even as it hollowed me out.

I convinced myself that if I just kept being righteous, if I kept believing and obeying, the hurt would go away. That my faith, devotion, and spiritual commitment would be enough. That God's promises of happiness, peace, and family would still come true. That if I stayed faithful enough, I could still have the life I had been taught to hope for.

That's why I didn't let myself grieve the loss of music. Not really. It was easier to call it faith than to admit I was heartbroken.

It didn't.

When I finally went back to graduate school to become a therapist, I thought I would finally gain clarity. By the time I finished, I had learned how to guide others through their emotions, but I still didn't think I had feelings of my own. Even as a therapist, I struggled to recognize or name what I was experiencing. I didn't understand how deeply my early life experiences and religious teachings had disconnected me from myself.

It wasn't until much later, when I began focusing on trauma work, that the pieces started to come together. For the first time, I began to see the full cost of what I had been taught. I realized how much I had silenced the parts of me that needed the most care. I had denied my own humanity in the name of faith, and I had built a pattern of ignoring myself that would take years to unravel.

Becoming Who Everyone Else Needed Me to Be

Growing up, I believed the rules would save me. I was taught that if I followed them, I would be loved. If I lived faithfully, I would belong. If I did everything "right," I would be rewarded, with friends, acceptance, and a family of my own. That family wasn't just a distant hope. It was central to how I understood my purpose and worthiness. Building a family was part of the promise, the plan, and the eternal dream I was taught to strive for.

But the rules came with conditions, ways I had to show up, ways I had to hide parts of myself. I was taught that my voice needed to be quiet and gentle. Questions weren't acceptable, and neither was being too bold, too assertive, or too much. I learned to temper myself, to suppress the energy and leadership that naturally bubbled to the surface. I learned to hold back the parts of me that didn't fit the mold. And it wasn't just my personality I was learning to suppress. I didn't yet understand the deeper parts of my identity and internal sense of worth, love, and belonging.

43

By the time I was a teenager, these lessons had taken root. I knew exactly how to dress, speak, and behave to meet the expectations of those around me. And yet, no matter how hard I tried, I still didn't feel like I belonged. I didn't fit in at church. I didn't fit in at school. I was always on the outside looking in, wondering what I was doing wrong. I remember begging my mom not to make me go to church on Wednesdays because I knew I didn't belong there. I'd go anyway because that's what you were supposed to do, and I'd try again to fit in. But nothing ever worked.

The disconnect wasn't just about rejection. It was about the promises I was raised to believe in, the idea that if I followed the rules, I would find love, friendship, and a family. I was doing everything I was supposed to do. I was faithful. I was obedient. I was quiet. But the rewards never came. That was the first crack, realizing that the promises weren't being fulfilled, even though I was keeping my end of the bargain.

As I reflect on that time now, I see how much of my identity was shaped by trying to fit into spaces that didn't value the fullness of who I was. I wasn't allowed to question, so I learned all the 'right' answers. I wasn't allowed to be loud, so I learned to be quiet. I wasn't allowed to lead, so I learned to follow. I wasn't allowed to ask for what I needed, so I learned to outsource my voice to others. And all the while, I kept believing that if I could just suppress enough of myself, if I could just become the person they wanted me to be, I would finally belong.

But I never did.

That longing for belonging, the deep ache of wanting to be seen, loved, and accepted, followed me for years. It wasn't until much later, when I began to unpack the layers of religious trauma that I realized how much of myself I had lost in the process. The rules didn't save me. They silenced me. And the cost of that silence was far greater than I could have understood at the time.

Earned Worth and Conditional Love

One of the most insidious parts of these teachings was the idea that my worth wasn't inherent. It was something I had to earn. I was taught that if I followed the rules, lived faithfully, and did everything "right," I would be worthy of love, belonging, and God's blessings. But if I failed, I wouldn't just lose those blessings. I'd lose my worth.

This belief shaped how I saw myself and others. Love wasn't unconditional; it came with requirements. I had to prove myself to God, my community, and even myself by being good enough, faithful enough, and obedient enough. But no matter how much I tried, it never felt like enough. The bar kept moving, and the harder I worked, the more it seemed I was falling short.

The most painful part was realizing how deeply I had internalized this idea of conditional love. It wasn't just that others were measuring my worth. I was doing it to myself. I believed that my value depended on how well I could perform, how much I could give, and how perfectly I could conform to the expectations placed on me.

It took me years to see how much that belief had stolen from me. How it had silenced parts of me, disconnected me from my needs, and left me feeling like I could never truly belong. Giving up music felt like the ultimate test of that belief. I thought I was proving my devotion. But worth didn't come. Peace didn't come. Just more silence.

Looking Back

When I look back now, I can see how these moments were all connected. Each one a piece of something bigger that I didn't have words for at the time. I didn't know how to explain the pain of walking away from music or the emptiness that followed when I kept doing all the "right" things and still felt so far from peace. I couldn't see yet how much I had learned to question myself instead of the system. How deeply I had believed that my feelings were wrong, that my voice didn't matter, and that my worth depended on how well I could shrink myself to fit what was expected.

But underneath all of it was something even heavier, the weight of the promises I had built my life around. A family on earth that would lead to eternal happiness. An eternal family. Exaltation. These weren't just spiritual hopes. They were the plan. The goal. The proof that I was doing it right. And I believed with everything in me that if I was faithful and I followed the path exactly, those promises would come true.

So I kept going. I told myself obedience would eventually bring peace. That if I could just stay the course, keep showing up, and keep shutting down the parts of me that didn't quite fit, it would all work out. That belonging was just one more act of faith away. But those promises, the ones I clung to, never came. And each time I tried to keep moving forward, I felt the ground beneath me start to give. The cracks were growing. And I didn't know how much longer I could keep pretending I didn't see them.

For a long time, I didn't let myself question any of it. Because it didn't feel like trauma. It felt like faithfulness. Like righteousness. Like doing what I was supposed to do. Trauma was what happened to other people. I just thought I was struggling to be good.

It wasn't until much later, after years of silence, striving, and disconnection, that I started to see it for what it was. The patterns were all there. Suppression. Disconnection. Betrayal. Religious trauma.

Suppression of my emotions, my voice, my identity. Disconnection from my worth, my needs, my sense of self. Betrayal. Not just by the promises I had trusted but by the system that told me my pain didn't matter as long as I was obedient.

At the time, I couldn't name it. I didn't have the language. But once I started untangling the harm, it became so clear. This wasn't just my personal struggle. It was a systemic one. It was what happens when you're raised inside a framework that promises everything, including peace, love, and salvation, if you'll just give up more and more of who you are.

Even after I saw it, the work of unraveling it had just begun. Naming the harm was only the first step. Learning how to find myself again, how to trust my voice, feel my feelings, and believe I was allowed to take up space would take years. Years of slow, intentional, often painful work.

I had been doing everything I knew to move toward healing. At least I thought I was. I became a therapist. I read the books. I sat with people in their pain. I believed that if I could understand it, I could overcome it. That if I talked about it enough, it would lose its grip.

But I stayed out of my own story. I stayed out of my body. Out of my pain. I thought knowing was the same as healing. But it wasn't. Not for me. Not for any of us.

Because healing doesn't happen in your head. It happens in your attachment. In your nervous system. In the patterns you live without realizing.

I had to find a tool that could reach the parts of me I had protected for so long. The part of me that was brilliant at thinking through pain but terrified to feel it. That's what trauma work, specifically EMDR, gave me. It helped me move past the protective part of my brain that kept me analyzing, intellectualizing, and staying safe through distance. It helped me stop just talking about my pain and start feeling it in my body, my breath, and the places I didn't even know I was still holding it.

I cried in ways I didn't know I could. I felt emotions I thought I wasn't allowed to have. And slowly, I started to connect with the younger versions of myself I had left behind. The ones who never got what they needed. The ones who thought it was their fault.

EMDR didn't give me all the answers. But it helped me find the parts of myself I had pushed away. The parts that didn't need to be fixed, just felt. Just seen. Just held with love and truth. It brought the unraveling pieces into the light, so I could begin to move forward. Not as someone trying to be whole but as someone already becoming.

Healing lives in the places that ache. The parts that hide. The moments when your body says no before your brain can explain why.

If you're starting to notice that your foundation doesn't quite feel like your own or that something isn't sitting right, those cracks you're seeing aren't proof that you're broken. They're signs that something deeper is calling to be seen. You don't need the words yet. You don't have to know what it means. Just noticing is enough. That is the beginning.

Your story might echo mine, or it might be entirely different. Either way, the work is the same.

Learning to listen. Learning to trust the quiet voice inside you. And learning to feel what you spent a lifetime avoiding.

It takes time. And you are allowed to take all the time you need.

This is where the next chapter begins. With the unraveling. With the patterns I didn't yet understand but that changed everything.

Part 2

The Space Between

Finesse Literary Press Ltd.

This is the space between. The part of the journey where your foundation begins to crack, and you start to see what was buried underneath. Not the foundation you chose but the one you were given. The one shaped by systems, silence, and expectations that felt like truth.

This is the time for awareness. For naming. For looking back with clearer eyes and beginning to understand what shaped you. It's where the truth rises, sometimes slowly, sometimes all at once, and where the questions begin to outgrow the answers.

In these chapters, I begin to name the patterns. The shared stories, the quiet wounds, the weight so many of us carry. I'll still tell stories. I'll still speak from lived experience. But I'll also begin to teach. To give shape to what has long lived unnamed.

Please give yourself grace and understanding here. Take care of yourself as you need. Pause. Soothe. Let what needs to rise gently. There is no right pace. Only your pace.

Chapter 4

The Patterns Beneath the Silence

Shared Stories of Loss and Longing

When I first began untangling my own story, I couldn't see it clearly. The trauma didn't announce itself. It came wrapped in expectations and smiles. It came disguised as goodness.

I didn't know how to name what had happened to me. I just knew I felt lost. The people-pleasing. The constant confusion about who I was. The way I couldn't feel my emotions or name my needs. The pressure to be good, to be better, to earn love by getting it right. It all felt like a personal failure. Like I was the problem. Like if I could just be more faithful, more righteous, it would finally click.

But before I began doing my own healing work, I was already a therapist. I was already holding space for others. And once I started seeing my own story clearly, I began to see it in them too.

The same people-pleasing. The same identity confusion. The same struggle to feel or trust emotions. The self-abandonment. The shame. The quiet suffering beneath the surface. Different lives, different details, but the same patterns kept showing up.

That's when it hit me. It wasn't just me.

And it wasn't just through my own healing that I came to understand this. I've sat with hundreds of stories now. Raw, real, holy stories. Women, men, and nonbinary people from every kind of background carried wounds that were so familiar I could feel them in my body. The specifics were different. But the pain? The confusion? The deep need to finally make sense of it all? That part was the same.

As I listened, I began to notice the patterns. The losses. The longings. The ache to belong and the cost of trying to fit. I interviewed people about their experiences with religious trauma, what it took from them, what it left behind, and what healing looked like.

And I started teaching other therapists how to see it too. Because this pain hides in plain sight. And once you know what to look for, you see it everywhere.

Religious trauma isn't just something that happens to a few people, it's built into the system. It's in the way we're taught to measure our worth, silence our questions, and cut off parts of ourselves just to belong. And even though each story is deeply personal, the patterns that show up are hauntingly familiar. Stories of longing. Stories of silence. Of trying so hard to do it right. Of losing yourself in the process.

This chapter is about those stories. It's about the common threads. What you start to see when you take a step back. It's about how religious trauma doesn't just live in individuals. It lives in relationships. In families. In entire communities. And it's about how naming it and finally saying, *this is what it is*, is the first step toward healing.

How Religious Systems Shape Identity

Religious systems don't just teach us what to believe; they teach us who we're supposed to be. From a young age, we're given a blueprint. Here's what makes you good. Here's what makes you worthy. Here's what your life should look like if you want to belong.

But it's not just about who you're *supposed* to be. It's also about who you're *not* allowed to be.

The messages come early and often. Do not be too much. Do not ask hard questions. Do not be angry, sexual, ambitious, queer, emotional, or unsure. Do not stand out too much. Do not take up too much space. The system does not just shape identity by what it praises. It also shapes it by what it punishes or ignores.

And so much of our identity gets built around those lines. Around obedience. Around conformity. Around becoming the kind of person the system says is valuable and hiding the parts it says are not. We're taught to align ourselves with the roles we're given, to be faithful, selfless, modest, clean-cut, kind, and quiet. And somewhere along the way, we start to believe that who we are isn't enough on its own. That we have to become something else to be worthy of love.

For many of us, this shaping happens so gradually, it feels normal. It feels like the truth. We don't realize we're slowly stepping away from our true selves, we just think we're doing what's right. What's expected. But over time, those expectations get inside us. They start to define us. And when who we are doesn't fit the mold, we don't question the mold; we question ourselves.

And when that sense of self is built around rules and roles and expectations, it can be terrifying to feel something start to crack. Because if your worth and belonging are tied to being a certain kind of person, what happens when something inside you no longer fits that version?

One woman said it like this:

> "There were moments when things just didn't sit right. When something felt off. But instead of trusting that feeling, I immediately turned it back on myself. I assumed *I* was the problem. That I wasn't trying hard enough, wasn't spiritual enough, wasn't good enough. So I pushed down the discomfort and told myself to do better. I need to read more, pray more, serve more. Anything to silence that feeling."

Her words echo what I've heard from so many others. For a lot of us, the framework of faith didn't just tell us how to live; it told us who we were *allowed* to be. And when something inside us didn't line up with that, we didn't make space for it. We buried it.

Over time, it becomes second nature. You start shaping yourself to fit what's expected without realizing you're doing it. You smile when you're supposed to. You say the right things. You show up in all the ways you're told are good and right. And underneath it all, a quiet belief starts to form. A belief that who you truly are isn't trustworthy. That it's not ok to be yourself. That if you want to be loved, you can't be all of you. You have to stay small, stay agreeable, stay *righteous*, no matter what it costs.

The Pattern of Earned Worth

One of the most damaging messages many of us internalized was that our worth wasn't truly inherent; it had to be earned.

We were told we were loved unconditionally, that we were children of God, valuable just as we were. But the actual experience of growing up in the Church told a different story. We learned that worth came from obedience. From sacrifice. From getting it right. That to be worthy of love, belonging, and spiritual safety we had to constantly prove ourselves.

This didn't always feel harsh. Sometimes it felt motivating, even comforting. But over time, that quiet pressure to *be enough* started shaping everything. It shaped how we showed up, how we related to others, how we felt about ourselves. And the harder we tried to earn it, the more it felt just out of reach, like no matter what we did, it was never quite enough.

Earned worth doesn't just shape how we see ourselves; it shapes how we *live*. When your value is tied to being good enough, obedient enough, and selfless enough, you learn to perform. To show up in the ways you're supposed to. To prove, over and over, that you're worthy of love. Of belonging. Of being seen.

Perfectionism becomes your norm. It stops being about trying your best and starts being about survival. Because if you mess up, if you fall short, it doesn't just feel like a mistake, it feels like *you* are the mistake. You start to believe something in you is broken. That if you could just try harder, be better, you'd finally feel okay. You'd finally feel *enough*.

And to keep that perfection going, we learn to abandon ourselves. It's not just about striving, it's about silencing. We push away what we need, what we feel, and who we are because those parts don't always fit. They're inconvenient. Complicated. Risky. And when your belonging feels conditional, it's safer to disconnect from yourself than to risk being rejected by everyone else.

So we shape-shift. We perform. We become who we think we're supposed to be. And we get really good at it. We give and give and give until we're so used to the striving, we don't even notice we're doing it anymore. It becomes automatic. Normal. Expected.

But deep down, the ache never really goes away. That quiet, persistent fear that we're still not enough. That if we stop performing, stop proving, everything will fall apart. So we keep going. Hoping that maybe, *finally*, if we just give a little more, be a little better, we'll finally feel worthy.

The Cost of Disconnection

The hardest part about this pattern is how invisible it can be. When you've spent your whole life striving for worth, love, and belonging, it just feels normal. It feels like what you're *supposed* to do. You don't even realize how far you've drifted from yourself until something breaks. Until the promises fall apart. Until the weight of it all becomes too much to carry.

And when that shift finally comes, it's not just disorienting; it's heart-breaking. Because suddenly, you can see it. The parts of yourself you silenced. The relationships you lost. The years you spent trying to earn what should've been yours all along. And with that seeing comes grief. Deep, aching grief for everything you gave up without even realizing it.

Her words echoed something I have heard from so many others-

> "I've spent so long trying to be everything for everyone else that I don't even know who I am anymore. I don't know what I like, what I want, or what I need. I don't even know how to use my own voice."

That's what this kind of disconnection does. It's quiet. It builds slowly. And then one day, you realize you've been living a life that isn't even yours.

We were told our worth was inherent. But the system we were raised in didn't teach us how to feel that worth, it taught us how to earn it. It taught us that worth was something we had to prove. That if we messed up, doubted, or didn't fit the mold, we had to work our way back into love. Back into belonging. Back into safety.

The cost of that kind of disconnection runs deep. It shows up in adulthood as anxiety, perfectionism, burnout, emotional shutdown, and self-doubt. It shows up in relationships where we don't know how to ask for what we need or even believe we're allowed to have needs in the first place. It leaves so many of us feeling ungrounded, unsure, and completely cut off from ourselves.

Healing means reclaiming that connection. Not just to worth but to *self*. And for many of us, that self has to be rebuilt, not just remembered. It means learning how to trust your voice. How to feel your own feelings. How to belong to *you*, not the version you had to become to be accepted but the version you buried along the way.

Suppression of Self

One of the most pervasive patterns in religious trauma is the suppression of self. The ways we learn to silence, shrink, or ignore the parts of us that don't fit the mold. And for many of us, that started young. We were taught how to dress, how to speak, how to act in ways that aligned with what was expected of us. And over time, those lessons became second nature. We stopped asking what we were giving up to stay faithful; we just tried harder to do it right.

In my own life, I learned early on that being "too much" wasn't acceptable. I was told my voice needed to be quiet and gentle. That my natural energy, my leadership, my intensity, my questions weren't appropriate. So I held back. I learned to shrink. I learned to be smaller, softer, quieter, more acceptable. Even when it didn't feel authentic. Even when it didn't feel like *me*.

And I've heard so many similar stories from others. People who buried parts of themselves, like their sexuality, their passions, their questions, out of fear.

One woman put it plainly, without flinching:

> "I knew I couldn't be gay and stay in my church, so I spent years pretending I wasn't. I buried that part of myself so deep it took years to even begin to unearth it."

Another shared how they stopped asking questions because every time they voiced a doubt, they were shut down. "Eventually," they said, "I just stopped. I told myself it wasn't worth it anymore."

This kind of suppression often feels like survival. When the stakes are belonging, love, or even salvation, it makes sense to shut things down. To hide. To protect yourself. But over time, the cost adds up. We lose touch with who we are. We start to believe those hidden parts are dangerous, shameful, or wrong. And that shame seeps into every part of our lives.

The hardest part? When you've been suppressing yourself for so long, it just feels normal. It feels like what you're supposed to do. It's only when the weight becomes unbearable that you start to realize how much of yourself you've lost.

Reclaiming those parts isn't simple. It takes more than just recognizing the harm. It takes intention, curiosity, and compassion. It means coming back into a relationship with the pieces you buried: your voice, your needs, your identity. And that's not easy. It's slow. It's messy. It can feel disorienting at first. But there's freedom on the other side. Because when you start to show up fully, not just the version that was allowed, you finally begin to feel whole.

You're Not Broken, and it's Not Your Fault

If you're reading this and recognizing yourself in these patterns, if you feel overwhelmed, confused, or even ashamed, you're not broken.

These messages started early. For many of us, they were there before we even had words. We absorbed them through stories, tone, silence, rules, praise, and punishment. We learned what was "good" and what wasn't. What was welcome and what needed to be hidden. And when something shapes you that early, it doesn't feel harmful, it just feels familiar. It feels like truth.

I've heard so many people say, "But my childhood was great. My parents were good. I don't remember anything traumatic happening." And they mean it. Their families were loving. Their parents did their best. There wasn't one big moment of harm, just a thousand quiet ones. A thousand moments of shrinking, silencing, and striving to be who they were supposed to be.

This isn't about blaming our families. Most of the time, they were passing down what they were taught. They were trying to help us succeed in the world as they understood it. They were navigating the same fears and expectations, often without even realizing it.

So, of course, it's been hard to see it. Of course, it's been hard to question it. Of course, it's taken time.

This chapter isn't about blaming ourselves or our families for how we survived. It's about seeing, really seeing, the systems and messages that shaped us. Because once you see it, you can begin to name it. And once you can name it, you can begin to loosen its grip.

This kind of healing takes time, compassion, and courage.

It's hard work. But it's real. And it matters.

Reflection:

Which of these patterns do you recognize in your story?

Where might you have learned to survive in ways that hid your real self?

Gentle Permission:

It is okay if you are only beginning to see the patterns now.

You are allowed to name what hurt you.

You are allowed to begin again.

Chapter 5

Becoming What They Needed

Roles, Shame, and the Breaking of the Body

O ur bodies and identities are not just personal. They're political, theological, and cultural. In the LDS Church, womanhood isn't simply a biological reality; it's a divine assignment with prescribed behaviors, expectations, and limitations. This chapter explores how these prescribed roles shape not just what we do but who we fundamentally believe ourselves to be.

From our earliest memories, we were taught what it meant to be a "good" girl, a righteous young woman, and, eventually, a faithful wife and mother. These weren't just suggestions, they were presented as eternal truths, divine commandments about our very nature and purpose. As we internalized these teachings, we often lost connection with our authentic selves in an effort to become what the Church, our families, and our communities told us to be.

The cost of this disconnection runs deeper than most of us realize. It affects not just our sense of identity but our relationship with our bodies, voices, autonomy, and worth. By examining these roles and their impact, we begin to see not just what we've lost but what might be possible when we reclaim the right to define ourselves.

The patterns we saw in the last chapter about disconnection, striving for worth, and suppressing our true selves take on a specific shape for Mormon women. We don't just lose our identity in a vague, universal way. We lose it through distinctly feminine expectations. Through roles that were defined for us before we were born. These broad patterns of religious trauma become something specific, something gendered, something that shapes not just what we do but who we're allowed to be.

The Roles We Inherited – Womanhood as Obedience

Some of the rules were spoken out loud. Most weren't.

We begin learning before we know we're learning. Long before we understand language or belief, we're absorbing the world around us. What we watch. What we see. What our parents say and don't say. What they do and don't do. It all teaches us something about what it means to exist in our body, in our family, in our role.

We learn what's acceptable and what's not. What gets praise and what gets silence. We learn how to act based on who gets attention and who gets dismissed. These early moments, stacked up day after day, form the foundation of our core beliefs about who we're supposed to be.

Before we had words for obedience or sacrifice, we already knew how to do it. Praise came when we were quiet, gentle, helpful. Correction came when we asked too many questions or made too much noise.

We were taught how to be women before we ever knew what that meant. Through Church songs, Relief Society whispers, and the quiet way our mothers sacrificed without ever naming it as loss. We learned that our value was in our service. Our softness. Our ability to absorb.

Be nurturing. Be gentle. Be supportive. Be good.

Don't take up too much space. Don't make it about you. Don't complain. Don't say no.

Even as girls, we watched the way women around us were praised for shrinking. For serving. For staying quiet. It was holiness in action. To deny yourself was to become who God needed you to be.

Some of us heard that explicitly: You are being raised to be a wife and a mother. Some of us never heard anything else.

We didn't choose those roles. We inherited them. From our mothers and grandmothers, many of whom didn't have choices either. Many of whom believed, with their whole hearts, that self-sacrifice was the path to heaven. And even if they didn't believe it, survival meant performing it.

We were told to build our house upon the rock. But it was someone else's rock. Someone else's house. Someone else's plan.

So when we talk about religious trauma, we can't start with us.

This is what we were trained for. From the Primary songs to the Relief Society lessons. From watching our mothers serve in silence to hearing our leaders testify that obedience would bring us joy. From temple covenants that asked us to give ourselves over to whispered encouragement to let our husbands lead. We were prepared to follow, trust, and shape our lives around someone else's authority.

I recall a woman who realized, only after her divorce, that her righteous submission left her unprepared even to open her own bank account. She told me, 'I trusted the system to keep me safe. It never occurred to me that it would leave me this helpless.' These patterns echo across generations. They live in our mothers' silences. In our grandmothers' sacrifices. In the survival strategies passed down like heirlooms.

My grandmother never questioned why she couldn't say no. My mother never wondered why her needs always came last. They didn't see it as trauma. They saw it as love. As faithfulness. As the way things were supposed to be.

I once worked with a woman who found her great-grandmother's journal. Page after page of exhaustion, confusion, and loneliness yet always ending with forced gratitude. Forcing herself to be grateful for her trials. Reading those words was like seeing her life reflected across a century. Nothing had changed. Not the expectations. Not the silencing. Not the struggle.

Breaking this cycle feels like betrayal, not just of the Church but of our mothers, our grandmothers, and all the women who endured quietly before us. Their suffering was sacred, their endurance praised as righteousness. To question this legacy doesn't just feel like doubting their faithfulness, it feels like jeopardizing their eternal salvation. Yet perhaps the greatest honor we can offer these women isn't to repeat their sacrifices but to liberate ourselves and them from patterns that never served us.

But what if the greatest honor we can give them isn't imitation but liberation?

We Lost Ourselves Trying to Be Good

We didn't just inherit the roles. We shaped ourselves to fit them. We were praised for how well we carried the emotional weight of our homes, for being calm, for smoothing conflict, for managing everyone else's needs without asking for anything in return.

We were also trained to prevent disappointment. To soften our words, anticipate reactions, and adjust ourselves so no one else would feel discomfort. Disappointment wasn't just unpleasant; it felt like failure. If someone around us was upset, we had done something wrong. We learned to read the room before we read our own emotions. We stayed small, agreeable, and flexible, not because it was who we were but because it kept the people we loved from feeling let down. We were taught that managing others' feelings, especially their disappointment, was part of our spiritual duty.

I've worked with so many women who lost themselves trying to be good. Women who never learned how to say no, who constantly served those around them until they had nothing left to give. They were exhausted. Overwhelmed. Stressed to the point they could barely function. And still, they pushed forward, helping everyone else while ignoring their own needs. The idea of taking a bath, resting, or saying, "I can't" felt selfish. Indulgent. Wrong.

Some had asked for help. Some had gone to their bishops in the middle of emotional or physical abuse, only to be told to stay. That if they were righteous enough, if they just held on, things would work out. That message wasn't just harmful; it was paralyzing.

We stopped asking what we wanted. We stopped wondering who we were. We started asking instead, what does God want from me? What does my husband need? What would a good mother do? A good woman? A righteous daughter?

Our choices were no longer about alignment with self. They were about alignment with expectation. These teachings weren't presented as options; they were givens.

And for a while, it worked. We got praise. We were seen as faithful, dependable, and kind. We served and volunteered and nurtured and stayed up late making casseroles for someone else's crisis while quietly drowning in our own.

We told ourselves this is what love looks like. This is what sacrifice means. This is how you become holy.

But something else was happening underneath.

We got smaller. More tired. More resentful. Some of us lost our voices. If we did use our voice, it was often ignored or dismissed in deference to a man's opinion. Some of us lost our health. Some of us lost the fire that used to burn in our bellies. We stopped knowing how to answer when someone asked what we wanted or needed. We didn't know how to even ask ourselves.

Because being good meant being quiet. Being good meant not making waves. Being good meant staying in the role, even when it stopped fitting.

And sometimes, we only realized what we lost when we started to wake up. When the edges began to fray. When the grief started to rise. When we whispered, "I don't think I ever got to be me."

This isn't just culture. It's survival. The constant people-pleasing. The hypervigilance to others' needs. The automatic dampening of our voices, our feelings, our presence. These aren't personality traits. They're trauma responses.

When authentic expression gets met with withdrawal, correction, or rejection enough times, the body learns. It adapts. It finds what works.

"I can feel my body change when I walk into church," one woman told me quietly "My voice gets softer. My posture shifts. My feelings shut down. It happens before I even think about it. My body remembers what's safe here and what isn't."

This adaptation follows us everywhere. Apologizing when someone bumps into us. Feeling responsible for everyone else's emotions. Anxiety that floods our bodies when we try to set even the smallest boundary.

What gets praised as "feminine virtue," such as selflessness, constant accommodation, and emotional caretaking, often reflects trauma adaptations wrapped in religious language. These adaptations form deep-rooted core beliefs about our worth, our role in relationships, and what we're allowed to need. Buried within our nervous systems, these schemas drive habitual coping strategies like surrender, avoidance, and overcompensation. They may protect us at first, but over time, they reinforce a sense of powerlessness.

Our Bodies as Temples, Threats, and Territories

"Your body is a temple."

Most LDS women have heard this phrase countless times. On the surface, it sounds empowering, our bodies are sacred, holy, divine. But the message rarely stopped there. The temple metaphor quickly became a means of control rather than reverence.

Because while our bodies were temples, they were also dangerous, not just to ourselves but to the men and boys around us. Our shoulders, knees, stomachs, and chests became battlegrounds of virtue, territories to be covered and controlled. The burden of others' thoughts wasn't just placed on our clothing choices; it was internalized as shame about our very existence in physical form.

I worked with a young woman who was told by her Young Women's leader that wearing a tank top to play basketball was "like leaving pornography on the table for your brother to find." She was thirteen. What she learned in that moment wasn't respect for her body; it was fear of it. She began to see her developing figure as something shameful, something that needed to be hidden, controlled, and constantly monitored.

Another client shared how she'd been pulled aside after sacrament meeting because her skirt, while reaching her knees when standing, revealed more of her legs when she sat down. The message was clear: her body was a constant problem to be managed, a potential stumbling block for the men around her, regardless of her intentions or comfort.

These weren't isolated incidents. They were part of a systematic approach to female embodiment, one that taught us to be hypervigilant about our physical presence while simultaneously disconnecting us from our own bodily experiences.

This disconnection went beyond modesty. It extended to how we related to desire, pleasure, pain, and autonomy. Many women I've worked with describe a profound alienation from their physical sensations, an inability to identify hunger, fatigue, or even pain because they were so accustomed to overriding their body's signals.

One woman in her forties shared that she'd never thought to question whether she enjoyed physical intimacy with her husband. "I knew it was my duty," she explained. "I never considered whether I wanted it or how it felt for me." Her body had become a site of service, not pleasure or personal experience.

The conditioning was so complete that many of us didn't even recognize it was happening. We believed we were making choices about modesty, sexuality, and physical boundaries when, in reality, we had internalized a system that made those choices for us long before we had the language to question them.

Reclaiming our bodies isn't just about changing how we dress or move through the world. It's about fundamentally shifting how we inhabit our physical selves, learning to listen to our bodies' wisdom rather than silencing it, honor our boundaries rather than abandoning them, and experience our physical existence as a source of personal power rather than potential sin.

The messages weren't subtle. They were everywhere.

Young Women's values: Divine Nature. Individual Worth. Knowledge. Choice. Accountability. Good Works. Integrity. Virtue. Words that sounded like empowerment but narrowed to a single path: modesty, motherhood, marriage. The medallion we earned wasn't a recognition of our unique gifts. It was confirmation that we could follow the template.

Relief Society: "Charity never faileth." But what they meant by charity was service. Sacrifice. Silence. The ability to give without needing in return.

Every General Conference, the pattern was the same. Talks to women emphasized modesty, gentleness, and supporting priesthood. Talks to men focused on authority, leadership, and decision-making. The contrast wasn't hidden. It was the point.

"For the Strength of Youth" pamphlets placed the burden of sexual purity on our shoulders. Our bodies became responsible for men's thoughts. Our clothes became worthy or unworthy, not based on comfort or expression but on how they might affect the boys around us.

Even the smallest weekly practices reinforced the hierarchy. Boys passed the sacrament. Men conducted meetings. Women could pray first but never last. These weren't accidents or local customs. They were designed. Intentional. A constant reminder of who held power and who didn't.

Covenants of Silence and Submission

For many of us, the expectations didn't stop at culture. They were codified in the temple, sanctified through ritual, symbolism, and sacred promises that bound us not just to God but to a specific understanding of divine order and feminine submission.

We were asked to make eternal promises. To give ourselves to our husbands. To obey them as they obeyed God. To serve, to follow, to sacrifice. It was framed as sacred. Divine. The order of heaven.

Even though temple language has softened in recent years, women carry internalized messages that persist long after external wording changes. Covenants of silence and submission became embodied truths, lingering beneath the surface, guiding decisions and relationships unconsciously.

I've sat with women who wept in the celestial room, trying to reconcile the ache in their bodies with the story they were being told. Others who tried to silence the discomfort, believing their doubts were spiritual weakness. But that discomfort was not doubt. It was knowing.

One woman described her first temple experience this way: "I felt like something broke inside me. Here I was, preparing for what was supposed to be the most sacred moment of my life, and suddenly, I was promising to give myself to my husband while he gave himself to God. I wasn't equal. I wasn't my own. But everyone around me looked so peaceful, so I thought the problem must be me."

Another shared how she'd gone back to her bishop after her endowment, troubled by what she'd experienced. "He told me I just needed to pray more, to seek understanding. That it would become beautiful to me if I was faithful enough." She spent years trying to silence her discomfort, believing her reaction was a spiritual failing rather than a legitimate response to a troubling promise.

Sacred vs. Silence

Sometimes the language of the sacred is used to sanctify silence. We are taught that certain things are too holy to question, too divine to challenge. Speaking about them, even in our own pain, is framed as rebellion or faithlessness.

But not everything labeled sacred is safe. Sometimes "protecting the sacred" is really about protecting power. It becomes a way to silence harm, to erase truth, to keep people small.

> Silence is a tool in abusive systems and relationships. It is used to maintain control, to protect those in power, and to keep those who are hurting from ever being heard.

The power of these covenants extends beyond the temple. They shape how women navigate disagreements in their marriages, how they approach decision-making, and how they understand their own spiritual authority. One client described how, during a significant family decision, her husband simply said, "Remember your covenants," when she disagreed with his choice. The conversation was effectively over; her eternal promises had become a tool to silence her voice.

These covenants didn't just shape belief. They shaped behavior. They shaped marriage. They shaped survival.

For many, they became the ultimate justification for enduring harmful relationships or situations. If you've promised before God to submit, follow, and give yourself over, then leaving, even when the relationship has become harmful, feels like breaking a sacred vow. Women describe staying in emotionally or physically abusive marriages because they believed God expected their endurance, silence, and sacrifice.

And when you've been taught that obedience is your holiness, it's no surprise that so many women gave everything, spiritually, emotionally, and financially.

The weight of these covenants isn't just in their content but in their context. Made in sacred spaces, surrounded by loved ones, with eternal consequences attached, they carry an authority that ordinary promises don't. Questioning them feels like questioning God himself. And for many women, that's a spiritual risk too great to take, even when those covenants have become chains rather than blessings.

The Paradox of Exaltation and Subordination

They tell us we're divine, and then they tell us to be silent.

This is the central contradiction of LDS womanhood. We're exalted in theory, subordinated in practice. We're told our spiritual nature makes us superior, more nurturing, more naturally Christlike, more spiritually attuned. Then that "superiority" becomes the very reason we can't lead, can't decide, can't question.

Motherhood is our priesthood, they say. Equal but different. But this equality never translates to equal voice, equal authority, equal power. We'll be goddesses someday, they promise. But don't ask what that means. Don't wonder why Heavenly Mother stays hidden, unnamed, unaddressed.

"I felt spiritually gaslighted," one woman explained to me. "I was told I had special gifts but was silenced whenever I tried to use them in ways that challenged anything."

Another couldn't reconcile being told her highest divine destiny was to become like someone who couldn't be named, discussed, or approached. "How can my ultimate goal be to become someone who's erased? It's like being told my divinity depends on my disappearance."

This contradiction traps us. When we question subordination, they remind us of our special nature, which becomes the very reason we should accept our limits. We're caught between rejecting our divine identity or accepting practical inequality as its price.

This isn't just confusing. It's a profound split in our sense of self. We're constantly reconciling our spiritual worth with our daily experience of limitation. The mental energy this takes is exhausting. And the system depends on it.

Specific Institutional Practices

It's not just culture. It's structure. It's policy. It's power.

Disciplinary councils: Men sit in judgment, even when the person being judged is a woman. Our most vulnerable, painful moments are examined entirely through male eyes, male perspectives, male authority.

Abuse cases: The system protects itself first. "Don't cause controversy," bishops counsel. "Forgive him." "Think of the damage to the Church's reputation." The institution shields priesthood holders who cause harm while women carry the wounds.

Temple recommend interviews: We discuss our most intimate worthiness with men who have power over our eternal standing. The discomfort, the vulnerability, the power imbalance, all of it becomes something else we're expected to silently endure.

Sunday worship: We watch boys pass the sacrament as the men bless it. We see men conduct meetings, give the final prayers, make the ultimate decisions. These aren't just symbolic differences. They're visible, weekly reminders of who can act and who must watch.

Even Relief Society, supposedly our organization, ultimately answers to priesthood authority. Our curriculum needs approval. Our activities need permission. Our budgets need male signatures. And when resources get allocated, women's programs get what's left after priesthood priorities are met.

These aren't just theological abstractions. They're concrete practices that shape how we understand our worth, our voice, our place. When every system and structure reinforces that men lead and women support, the message doesn't need to be spoken aloud. It's built into the foundations.

The Cost of Trusting the System

This is what we were trained for.

From the Primary songs to the Relief Society lessons. From watching our mothers serve in silence to hearing our leaders testify that obedience will bring us joy. From the temple covenants that asked us to give ourselves over to the whispered encouragement to let our husbands lead.

We were prepared to follow. To trust. To shape our lives around someone else's authority.

And for many women, that trust became the foundation of everything: spiritually, emotionally, financially, intellectually, and physically.

Spiritual Cost

When our connection to God is mediated through priesthood leadership, we lose direct access to our own spiritual authority. Many women I've worked with describe feeling like they needed permission to receive personal revelation, especially if it contradicted what a priesthood leader had said. One woman shared how she'd felt strongly prompted to decline a calling, but when her bishop insisted it was God's will, she accepted it despite her misgivings. The resulting anxiety and burnout left her questioning not just the calling but her ability to hear God's voice at all.

Emotional Cost

The emotional labor of maintaining peace, absorbing others' feelings, and silencing our own needs exacts a tremendous toll. I remember one client who spent decades managing her husband's emotions, ensuring the house was perfect when he came home, the children were quiet when he needed rest, and her feelings were never "too much" for him to handle. When she finally began therapy, she couldn't identify a single emotion. She was "fine" and numb. Everything she felt was filtered through how it might affect others, leaving her emotionally exhausted and disconnected from herself.

Financial Cost

I interviewed one woman who had followed the LDS teachings exactly. She deferred to her husband in every major decision. Trusted him to manage their money, their home, their future. That, she had been taught, was her divine role: to support him. To sustain him. To create peace while he presided. And then, one day, he left.

She was left with no savings. No job. No experience managing her own resources. No sense of how to survive outside the role she had been praised for fulfilling. "I didn't even know where to start," she told me. "I trusted him because I believed I was supposed to. Because I believed God wanted me to."

Another woman, married for thirty years, discovered her husband had been hiding significant debt while maintaining complete control of their finances. When she confronted him, he quoted scripture about wives being submissive and reminded her of her temple covenants. Her bishop counseled patience and forgiveness rather than financial independence.

Intellectual Cost

The cost extends to intellectual autonomy as well. Many women describe being taught that questioning doctrine or policy was dangerous, a sign of pride or lack of faith. One client, a brilliant woman with a passion for theology, spent years hiding the books she read and the questions she explored. "I was afraid of being seen as unfaithful," she explained. "I thought my curiosity was something to overcome. It was a weakness and not something to value. Questioning wasn't just discouraged; it was framed as a threat to my very faith." This intellectual suppression didn't just affect her relationship with the church. It shaped how she approached every aspect of life, always deferring to others' expertise rather than trusting her mind.

Physical Cost

Perhaps most intimate is the physical cost of trusting the system. Women learn that their bodies exist primarily for others, for bearing children, for pleasing husbands, for maintaining a certain standard of modesty and appearance. One woman shared how she ignored severe pain for years because she'd been taught that motherhood was supposed to involve sacrifice. Another described feeling she had no right to say no to intimacy, believing it was her divine duty to prioritize her husband's desires above her own needs, comfort, or even her consent.

This isn't just about financial hardship or emotional burden. It's about spiritual conditioning. It's about how belief systems create practical vulnerability. About how theological submission becomes structural dependence. About how the roles we were asked to inhabit leave us without ground to stand on when those roles fall apart.

And then we're the ones who carry the shame. The blame. The struggle. And the system that shaped us remains untouched.

So many women internalize the belief that dependence is divine. That needing less makes you holier. That trusting someone else to lead is not just virtuous but required. And by the time they start to question it, they've built entire lives around a version of goodness that never included their voice.

The journey back to trusting ourselves, our spirits, emotions, minds, and bodies often begins with the painful recognition of what that trust in the system has cost us. This isn't just about individual choices or relationships. It's about a system designed to keep women dependent, praise submission as divinely ordained, and frame autonomy as selfishness or rebellion.

Recognizing these costs isn't about placing blame. It's about beginning to understand the full scope of what we've carried, often silently, and what healing might require.

Resistance and Resilience

Even inside these narrow roles, women found ways to resist. Small ways. Hidden ways. Ways that preserved something essential without risking everything.

Some found it in friendships with other Relief Society sisters, connections that went deeper than the lessons that offered understanding no one else could give. Some found it in journals, where they could finally say what they couldn't speak aloud. Some found it in scripture, discovering passages that affirmed their worth in ways that contradicted everything they'd been taught.

"I looked like the perfect Mormon woman," one client told me, "but inside, I was constantly filtering, questioning, holding onto myself. They couldn't take what they didn't know was there."

Another created a tiny space of power in how she gave prayers, speaking with authority even when authority wasn't given to her. Another taught lessons that gently pushed against traditional interpretations. Small moments of authenticity. Quiet rebellions that no one else might notice.

These weren't grand gestures. They were survival. They were the ways women protected some small part of themselves when everything else had to be surrendered. They didn't change the system. But they kept something alive inside it.

Reclaiming What Was Taken

The roles we inherited weren't just about behavior; they were about identity. They defined who we were allowed to be, how we were permitted to move through the world, and what parts of ourselves were welcome. They shaped not just our choices but our sense of possibility.

But understanding these patterns isn't about assigning blame. It's about seeing clearly what has shaped us so we can make conscious choices about who we want to become. It's about recognizing that while we may have been taught that our worth comes from obedience, our value was never dependent on how well we could conform.

The journey of reclaiming ourselves after religious trauma isn't linear or simple. It often begins with grief, mourning the self we never got to be, the voice we never got to use, and the life we might have lived had we been taught to trust ourselves as much as we were taught to trust authority.

But grief isn't the end of the story. It's the beginning of something new. As we untangle these inherited roles, as we question the foundations they were built on, we create space for authentic identity to emerge. Not the self that was prescribed to us but the self that has been waiting all along.

In the next chapter, we'll explore how these gender-based expectations intersect with other aspects of identity, race, sexuality, class, and ability, creating complex layers of harm and healing. Because the roles we've discussed don't impact all women equally, understanding these differences is essential to creating paths toward wholeness that honor our full humanity.

Reflection:

What roles were you taught you had to play to be good, worthy, and loved?

Where did those roles ask you to abandon yourself?

Permission:

You are allowed to come home to your body.

You are allowed to exist without apology.

Chapter 6

Layer Upon Layer

Intersectionality and the Depth of Religious Trauma

R eligious trauma doesn't happen in isolation. Teachings like modesty, submission, and emotional labor affect many people raised in traditional religious structures, but the way those teachings land is shaped by the identities we carry. Gender, race, sexual orientation, socioeconomic status, neurodivergence, and so many other parts of who we are influence how we experience harm and how we are seen or unseen within the system.

A woman might take modesty teachings as a message to shrink herself and disconnect from her sexuality. A transgender or nonbinary person might experience the same teaching as a denial of their very existence. A white woman may be praised for her obedience and sacrifice, while a woman of color may be overlooked, misread, or expected to prove her devotion in ways others are not. These are not surface-level differences. They reveal how systems reward certain bodies and silence others.

This chapter is not a full or final account of these intersections. It's a starting place. An invitation to notice where harm shows up in layers. To begin recognizing how trauma is shaped by culture, identity, and systems of power. If you want to go deeper, start by listening. Not to respond or to explain but to understand. That kind of listening creates space for stories that haven't been told. It creates space for healing.

Some of the most painful erasure happens when religion teaches people that who they are is inherently wrong.

LGBTQIA2S+ Experiences

The experiences of LGBTQIA2S+ individuals within religious systems reveal profound, often hidden layers of harm. Religious teachings frequently frame diverse identities as sinful, creating environments where people feel erased, excluded, or vilified simply for being themselves. Although these harms can overlap, the experiences of those navigating gender identity differ in important ways from those navigating sexual orientation. This section explores these themes, highlighting the harm caused by rigid teachings and the resilience found along paths of healing.

Gender and Religious Trauma

Religious teachings around gender are often presented as divine design; they define clear roles, sacred duties, and eternal identities. For many people, these roles become the foundation of how they understand themselves, relationships, and place in the world. But when those roles are rigid, narrow, or absolute, they can become painful containers. Instead of offering guidance, they become rules that leave little room for difference, complexity, or growth.

For nonbinary and transgender individuals, that pain runs even deeper. Many are never included in the story at all. Religious frameworks that define people strictly as men or women, each with assigned spiritual roles, leave no space for those whose identities exist outside that binary. The result is often invisibility, rejection, and the belief that something about them is inherently wrong.

This erasure isn't passive. It's built into the system. Whole teachings, policies, and roles are structured in a way that exclude nonbinary and transgender people entirely. Their existence is framed as sinful, broken, or unnatural. One nonbinary person put it this way: "I grew up believing people like me weren't supposed to exist. It wasn't just a lack of representation. It was a complete denial of my identity. I had to ignore who I was in order to be righteous."

For many, the fear of coming out is not just emotional; it is survival. Revealing their identity often means being removed from leadership, losing family relationships, and being pushed out of the very communities they grew up in. For transgender individuals, the risk can feel even higher, especially when transitions are visible and invite public scrutiny. One trans woman said, "I knew the moment I told them who I was, I would lose everything. My family, my friends, my faith. My parents would choose the church over me. And I wasn't sure I could survive that." That kind of fear doesn't just lead to silence. It leads to self-erasure. To shrinking, pretending, and surviving at the cost of authenticity.

The emotional toll is heavy. Nonbinary and transgender people raised in religious systems often carry profound anxiety, depression, and thoughts of self-harm. The constant message that their identity is wrong leads to deep shame and isolation. It becomes hard to trust, hard to feel safe, and hard to imagine that healing is even possible.

But healing does happen. It often begins with reclaiming identity, slowly and deliberately, in a way that feels safe. It begins when people find spaces that reflect their truth. Not spaces that tolerate them but spaces that celebrate them. That process doesn't look the same for everyone. Some redefine their spirituality. Some walk away and build something entirely new. And some choose to stay. They stay in the church. They stay connected to their faith. They stay rooted in something that once caused harm, but now they see it with open eyes. They set boundaries. They claim their place with more clarity and less fear.

At its core, healing means stepping out of shame and into self-acceptance. It means releasing the belief that there was ever something wrong with who they are. It means choosing to live fully, whether that path leads them further in, further away, or somewhere that hasn't been named yet. It means being seen, not just by others but by themselves.

Sexuality and Religious Trauma

Many of us were taught that sexuality was a sin, and if our sexuality didn't fit the mold, then something was wrong with us. Being gay, lesbian, or bisexual wasn't just framed as different. It was framed as sinful. Same-sex attraction was called a temptation. A test. A burden. We weren't taught to see love as sacred. We were taught to fear it.

That message shaped everything. It showed up in talks and interviews. It was tucked into the language of "same-sex attraction" and "living the gospel despite your feelings." It was in the quiet expectation that if you were queer, your highest calling was to suffer silently. To stay single. To live without intimacy and pretend that was righteous.

One woman said, "I thought there was something fundamentally flawed about me, like I was a mistake in God's eyes. It took years to realize I wasn't broken. The system was."

This harm doesn't stay abstract. It settles deep in the body. It fractures self-worth. It teaches people to separate from their hearts. Many are expected to deny their need for love, connection, and touch. And when they do try to connect, it's with fear in their chest and shame in their bones. They're told that loving someone in the way that feels most true is evidence of failure.

The conflict between faith and identity can create constant grief. Another woman told me, "I felt like I didn't belong anywhere. I wasn't enough for the church, but I didn't know how to be myself outside of it." That limbo becomes a place of pain. There is no home in faith, no guide outside of it, just the ache of trying to be whole without a foundation.

Spiritual bypassing only adds to the harm. Phrases like "hate the sin, love the sinner" or "affirm the person, not the behavior" are offered as compassion. But they carry a sharp edge. They say, "We'll love you but only if you disappear." These words sound kind, but they teach people that their existence is something to be tolerated, not cherished. Over time, they learn that they are not fully allowed to show up as their true selves.

Conversion therapy deepens that harm. Often framed as healing, it tells people that safety, love, and salvation are only available if they reject who they are. Survivors often describe conversion therapy as deeply traumatizing, leading to significant mental health challenges and a lifetime of pain. They carry the trauma of being told that their truth made them unlovable. That their survival depended on being something they weren't.

This harm doesn't stay personal. It fractures families. Parents are told to choose the church over their children. One client shared, "My parents told me they loved me, but they couldn't accept who I was. I wasn't asking them to change their faith. I was asking them to choose me. And they couldn't." That rejection echoes long after the moment. It becomes a pattern of loss, of silence, of being loved with conditions.

Religious teachings about sexuality don't just exclude. They erase. They distort. They wound. But healing is possible. It begins with telling the truth. It begins with naming what was lost and what was never allowed to exist. It means honoring the right to desire, to love, to be held. It means reclaiming identity, voice, and belonging.

That path doesn't look the same for everyone. Some people leave completely. Some stay connected to parts of their faith while discarding the shame. Some rebuild a new kind of spirituality that makes space for all of who they are. And some stay. They find a way to remain that feels true to them, whether that means staying under the radar or creating space for themselves within the system. They stay with boundaries. With clarity. With the right to belong on their own terms.

Meet Brielle

She was the kind of girl who got everything right. Modest. Obedient. Devoted. She served a mission, married a returned missionary, and was known for her strength and testimony. No one ever questioned her. She didn't even question herself, not at first. She knew there was something different about her, but she assumed everyone felt that way. She didn't have any experience to compare it to. And besides, she was doing everything right.

She was gay. But she didn't know. Or maybe she did, somewhere deep down. But she had been so good at staying abstinent, so good at following the rules, that no one ever saw through it. Not even her.

It wasn't until much later, years into her marriage, that the pieces started to surface. The disconnection. The quiet grief. The parts of her she had never explored because they didn't fit the narrative she had been praised for. Coming out wasn't dramatic. It was slow. Painful. Quiet. She didn't lose her family. She didn't get disowned. But she did lose the version of herself that had been so carefully built for survival.

What made it so devastating wasn't that she had sinned. It was that she had succeeded. She had been celebrated for a life that erased her. For fitting into a story that never had room for who she truly was. And when she finally saw it, there was grief. Grief for the years spent performing. Grief for the love she never let herself feel. Grief for the girl who had always known, even if she couldn't say it.

Her story is one of thousands. Not all are the same, but the patterns echo. Queer people in religious systems are taught not just to deny desire but to erase identity. Women, in particular, are rewarded for how well they disappear. For being virtuous, supportive, obedient, and good. If they don't "act on it," they are praised. If they speak up, they are warned. And when they finally break the silence, it is often framed as betrayal, not liberation.

Healing for LGBTQIA2S+ people raised in faith systems means reclaiming the self that was silenced. It means honoring what was lost and, sometimes, what was never allowed to emerge at all. It doesn't always mean leaving the faith. It doesn't always mean coming out publicly. But it always means coming home to yourself, on your terms, in your own time.

Race, Cultural Identities and Religious Trauma

For people of color raised in predominantly white religious systems, the trauma is layered. It is the pain of exclusion, the pressure to assimilate, and the quiet erasure of identity, all wrapped in the language of love. The LDS Church, like many others, has a long history of racial exclusion. And while some policies have changed, the impact of those policies and teachings does not just disappear.

Many members of color grow up never hearing this history until much later. They are taught that the church is true, the leaders are divinely guided, and everything happens for a reason. And then one day they find out about the priesthood and temple bans. About the framing of Blackness as a curse. About the justifications that lingered long after 1978. One woman said, "I had always believed the church was true. Learning about the priesthood ban shattered something in me. How could God be part of a system that saw people like me as less?"

The betrayal runs deep. It's not just about what was taught. It's about what was never said. The silence. The erasure. The fact that no one warned them, no one acknowledged it, and no one made space to grieve or question. And when they do ask questions, they're often told to have faith. To stop being divisive. To focus on unity instead of history.

Whiteness is centered everywhere, in leadership, imagery, and culture. Jesus is white. Prophets are white. The examples of righteousness are white. Members of color are expected to adapt, fit in, and be grateful.

Expectations around language, dress, and behavior reflect white, middle-class norms. Fitting in often means shrinking parts of yourself.

For adoptees of color, the disconnection can be even more profound. Raised in white families, in white wards, in white communities, many are never given the language or tools to understand their own identity. One Korean adoptee shared, "I wasn't taught anything about where I came from. My culture didn't matter. My history didn't matter. I was just supposed to be grateful I was saved." That kind of narrative doesn't just ignore identity; it erases it.

Adoption practices within the LDS Church have long mirrored white saviorism. Children of color are often placed in white families with the assumption that this is a blessing. That love is enough. That culture, ancestry, and belonging are secondary to salvation. One adoptee said, "The message was clear. Whiteness was the goal. Being like them was the success story."

Meet Christy

> She was adopted as an infant by a white LDS family and raised in a predominantly white Utah ward. She followed every rule. Bore her testimony. Did everything right. And she was praised for how well she fit in. People called her "special" and "chosen." But no one ever asked what it felt like to never see herself reflected. No one talked about race. No one acknowledged what she had lost.

Her Blackness was visible but invisible. Her name before adoption, her heritage, her birth family, none of it was part of the story the church told her about herself. Her family believed their love should be enough. But for her, it wasn't.

As she got older, her body no longer allowed her to blend in. She was curvier than her sisters. Taller. Her shorts were called immodest, even when they were the same as everyone else's. She was pulled aside at youth activities. Judged more harshly. Teased for her hair. Called dramatic for crying. Called aggressive for standing up for herself. She began to shrink herself.

It wasn't until college that she began to unravel the cost of that silence. The cost of belonging that required her to disappear. When she finally named it out loud, people told her she was being too sensitive. That she was loved. That she was lucky. But their love had required her to disconnect from herself. And she could not carry both truths anymore.

For many members of color, the pressure to perform gratitude becomes a weight they carry alone. They are asked to represent diversity while conforming to white standards. Praised for being "well-spoken." Held up as examples of progress. But only as long as they don't make anyone uncomfortable. As long as they don't challenge the system that never saw them fully to begin with.

One Black LDS woman told me, "I was praised for how well I fit in. But fitting in meant erasing myself. I started to wonder if the parts of me that didn't fit were even allowed to exist."

Healing begins with naming that harm. With acknowledging that the church's history of exclusion is not over. It's still present in the culture. In who holds power. In who gets heard. In who gets believed.

For some, healing looks like reclaiming their culture, language, and voice. For others, it means stepping away from systems that never made room for them. For many, it means both.

Whatever it looks like, it starts with this: your story matters. Not because you were "chosen," not because you endured. But because you are whole. And your wholeness was never supposed to be negotiable.

Socioeconomic Status and Religious Trauma

In the LDS Church, teachings about tithing, self-reliance, and stewardship are often framed as spiritual principles. But for people living in financial stress, those teachings can turn into shame. They're told to give ten percent no matter what. That paying tithing first will bring blessings. That God will provide. And when the money still doesn't stretch, when bills pile up and food runs out, the message becomes personal. They didn't have enough faith. They didn't try hard enough. They weren't righteous enough to be blessed.

One woman shared, "I was told that if I paid my tithing, everything else would work out. But it didn't. I paid it anyway and still couldn't buy groceries. I thought it was my fault."

In communities where success is linked to righteousness, poverty becomes a sign of failure. People who are struggling don't just feel poor. They feel unseen. They feel like they don't belong. They show up at church hoping for comfort and are instead reminded, through talks, through quiet judgment, through who is called to lead, that they are not enough.

And when they ask for help, support is often conditional. One woman shared that after months of trying to get by, she finally went to her bishop for assistance. He denied her because she hadn't paid a full tithe. "I wasn't trying to cheat the system," she said. "I just didn't have enough. And instead of helping, they made me feel like I didn't deserve it."

For many women, the harm goes even deeper. They are encouraged to stay home, raise children, and rely on their husbands. And when that structure falls apart through death, divorce, or abandonment, they're left with nothing. No income. No retirement. No path forward. "I did everything I was told to do," one client said. "I stayed home with the kids. I supported my husband. And when he left, I had no job, no savings, and no support. I felt abandoned by the church that told me this was the right path."

The harm isn't just about money. It's about identity. About being seen as worthy only when you can perform. When you can give. When you look like success.

Healing from this kind of harm begins with questioning those messages. With naming the lie that wealth is a sign of faith and that struggling means you're doing something wrong. It means untangling your worth from your income. Letting go of the belief that you have to earn help. It means finding communities where your needs are not shameful. Where you don't have to buy your way into belonging.

And most of all, it means this: you were never less faithful because you struggled. You were never more righteous because you gave. Your worth is not up for negotiation. You deserve care, even when you have nothing to give.

Mental Health, Disability, and Neurodivergence in Religious Spaces

Disability. Neurodivergence. Mental health. These parts of the human experience are rarely named in religious spaces, and when they are, they're often spiritualized or dismissed. Most churches, including the LDS Church, aren't built with these bodies or minds in mind. And when you move through the world differently, when you think, feel, or process in ways that don't fit the expected mold, the message is clear: keep up, stay quiet, and don't make it anyone else's problem.

Many people learn early to hide the parts of themselves that don't fit. They mask. They perform. They study the rules so well they can pass as fine. They learn to smile. To sit still. To push through. Survival becomes the goal, not authenticity. And survival isn't the same as belonging.

This section is about what happens when those with different minds and bodies try to find belonging in spaces that were never built for them. It's about the harm of invisibility. The weight of performance. And what it means to finally stop trying to prove you deserve to be there.

Disability and Religious Trauma

The LDS Church often talks about love, inclusion, and divine worth. But the way it treats disabled people often tells a different story. Teachings about being "made whole" in the afterlife are framed as hopeful, but they carry another message too. They suggest that disability is something to overcome. Something temporary. Something flawed.

One woman said, "It made me feel like I was broken. Like the real me, the me God actually loved, would only exist after this life."

That framing turns disability into a test, a burden, a symbol. Disabled people are praised for their strength and faith. They're turned into inspiration. But not seen for who they are. They're asked to endure instead of being supported. And when they struggle, the response is spiritual, not practical.

Church buildings are often inaccessible. Leadership roles demand energy and schedules that many disabled members can't meet. Youth activities aren't designed with every body in mind. And even when someone asks for help, it often doesn't come. "I felt like I was burdening everyone just by being there," one woman said. "Every time I asked for something, it felt like I was interrupting the flow. Like I was the problem, and they only had to fix it because I was there. They didn't know how to include me, and after a while, I stopped trying."

Another woman told me she had to ask for the same accommodations almost every time she went to a meeting or gathering. Nothing was remembered. Nothing was planned for. It was always on her to speak up, advocate, and explain. "It was exhausting," she said. "It felt like I was always the one disrupting things, always the one making it harder." One day, someone told her, "It's just easier when you're not here." And that was it. That sentence stayed with her. The message wasn't subtle. Her presence was the problem.

The erasure isn't always cruel. Sometimes it's praise. "You're so strong." "You're such an example." "You're teaching all of us." But being someone else's lesson is not the same as being loved. It's lonely. It puts distance between you and the people who claim to care. It tells you that your value is in your suffering, not in your presence.

And then there are the caregivers. Mostly women. Mothers. Sisters. Wives. They show up every week carrying snacks, wheelchairs, calming tools, medical bags. They are praised for their patience, their sacrifice, their faith. But not supported. Not heard. Their burnout is spiritualized. Their exhaustion is framed as devotion.

Marcie had spent years bringing her son to church, balancing his needs with the expectations placed on her. Every Sunday she packed extra snacks, noise-canceling headphones, and backup clothes, just in case. She'd spend half the meeting walking the halls with him, calming meltdowns, trying to keep him regulated while still catching bits of the talks through the chapel doors. People told her all the time how inspiring she was. "You're amazing," they'd say. "So strong. So faithful." But no one offered to help. No one sat next to her on the bench or asked what she needed. "They saw me as a symbol of strength," she said. "But not as a person. Not as someone who was falling apart." And because everyone saw her that way, she didn't feel like she had permission to be honest about how hard it really was. It didn't seem like anyone would have heard her anyway. They had already decided who she was supposed to be.

This is what systemic ableism looks like in a spiritual space. You belong as long as your needs don't disrupt the structure. You're valued as long as you inspire others. You're loved as long as you don't ask for too much.

Healing from this harm begins with telling the truth. You are not broken. Your needs are not shameful. Your body and your mind are not spiritual flaws. Inclusion should not be conditional. Your worth was never supposed to depend on performance or suffering. You are already enough.

Neurodivergence: Autism and ADHD

Neurodivergence is a word that speaks to the natural diversity of how brains work. It includes identities like autism, ADHD, Tourette's, dyslexia, sensory processing differences, and others. It also includes mental health conditions like OCD, trauma, bipolar disorder, and more. Some people have formal diagnoses. Others just know they've always been different. Their minds move fast, slow, or all over the place. They feel everything deeply. They miss what others notice and notice what others miss. And they've spent their whole lives trying to keep up in a world that wasn't built for them.

Religious systems, especially those built around sameness and obedience, are often rigid and unforgiving for neurodivergent people. They don't leave room for questions, pacing, and differences. They reward those who perform well and discipline those who can't. And for people who are neurodivergent, that often means living in a constant state of internal correction. Don't interrupt. Don't stim. Don't be loud. Don't move. Don't forget. Don't speak out of turn. Don't ask why.

This section focuses specifically on autism and ADHD because these are not only common neurodivergent identities but also areas I specialize in both professionally and personally. This is my lived experience. These are also the stories I hold every day in my work.

Autistic Experiences

Autistic people often find a sense of comfort in structure and predictability. In some ways, religious life can feel like it fits. The rules are clear. The routines repeat. The expectations are laid out. That kind of structure can feel like a relief in a world that often moves too fast and doesn't make sense. But what starts off feeling safe can quickly become something else. When there's no room for questions, difference is framed as disobedience, and connection depends on doing everything the right way, the structure starts to suffocate. People might praise autistic folks for memorizing scripture or following rules, but they rarely ask how they're actually doing. Sensory needs get brushed off.

Honest questions are seen as distractions. Emotions are misread. The system might look steady, but that doesn't mean it's safe.

Autistic kids are often disciplined not just for acting out but for being themselves. They're told not to stim, not to fidget, not to make any noise. They're expected to sit still, make eye contact, smile at the right time, and never interrupt. If they hyperfocus on something that doesn't feel spiritual enough, they're redirected. If they don't participate in the social rituals the way everyone else does, they're seen as resistant. Their boundaries get crossed in the name of love. Their discomfort gets labeled as irreverence. Over time, those messages don't just teach them how to act. They teach them to shut it all down. To mask. To disconnect from their instincts. To perform belief instead of actually feeling it.

For autistic women, it's even harder to be seen. Many of them fly under the radar because they don't show up in the ways people expect. They're quiet. Obedient. Righteous. But what often looks like being easy is actually masking. It's survival. They learn early that their job is to keep the peace, make others comfortable, and do everything right without asking for too much. In religious spaces, that pressure gets spiritualized. They're praised for being reverent, humble, and selfless, even when they're barely holding it together. They memorize the right words. They play the part. They learn how to stay small. When they finally hit a wall, they're told it's a lack of faith. Most never hear the word autism until much later, if ever. Instead, they carry a quiet belief that they are the problem. That if they could just try a little harder, be a little better, they might finally belong.

ADHD Experiences

For people with ADHD, religious life often feels like a constant mismatch. Long meetings. Passive listening. Endless rules that no one says out loud but everyone is expected to follow. It's not just hard to keep up. It feels like you're constantly falling short. While other kids are praised for being reverent and still, kids with ADHD are often called out for fidgeting, forgetting, getting distracted, or speaking out of turn. They're not just corrected. They're spiritually reprimanded. Told to try harder. To pray more. To repent for not paying attention. They learn early that their brain is a problem. That their struggles aren't just frustrating. They are seen as moral failings.

Girls and women with ADHD often go completely unnoticed. Their inattention is interpreted as laziness. Their impulsivity is called dramatic. Their emotional sensitivity is seen as weakness. Many are praised for being sweet and helpful, even as they are working overtime to hold it all together. They mask their executive dysfunction with perfectionism. They mask their overwhelm with people-pleasing. They do everything they can to look like they are doing fine. And when it finally becomes too much and they break down or shut down, it is framed as a spiritual crisis. Or worse, a lack of faith.

The real story is never told. No one sees the effort. No one sees how hard they have been trying to meet impossible expectations in a system that was never built for their brain. And when they cannot keep up, they are not met with compassion. They are met with shame.

I didn't know I had ADHD until well into adulthood. I had spent years holding everything together or trying to. I knew I was exhausted.

I knew I couldn't focus the way other people seemed to. I was always running behind, losing things, trying to track conversations while my brain jumped ahead or spun in circles. But I also knew how to look like I was "FINE." I had learned that in church and everywhere in Utah. If I sat still, smiled, took notes, and bore my testimony the right way, no one questioned me. If I volunteered, said yes, stayed quiet, and showed up on time, they called it strength.

What they didn't see was the masking. What they didn't see was how hard I was working just to keep up. How guilty I felt every time I couldn't. I believed it was a spiritual problem. That's what I had been taught. If I prayed more, read more, focused more, I wouldn't feel so scattered. But it never worked. And when it didn't, I assumed the problem was me. I was too much.

It wasn't until years later that I started to understand. My brain wasn't broken. The overwhelm wasn't a weakness. I wasn't failing. I was surviving a system that was never built for me. Getting that language didn't fix everything, but it changed my story. It gave me back parts of myself I had spent years shaming into silence.

Healing for neurodivergent people often begins with unlearning the idea that their way of being is wrong. It means recognizing that their needs are real. Their ways of thinking, moving, processing, and feeling were never spiritual flaws. They never lacked faith. They were never too much or not enough. The harm came from being forced to fit a mold that was never built for them. Healing looks like letting go of that mold. It looks like moving their body when they need to. Taking breaks without guilt. Asking questions without shame. It looks like reclaiming the parts of themselves they were told to hide and finding belonging, not through performance but through being fully, beautifully who they are.

It looks like giving yourself back the grace you were never offered. Like telling the younger version of you that she was never broken. Just never supported.

Intersectionality as a Lens for Healing

As I look back at the stories shared in this chapter, what stands out most is how deeply interconnected everything is. These layers of identity, race, gender, sexuality, neurodivergence, disability, and class don't exist in isolation. They overlap, stacking on top of one another, creating complexities that shape the harm people experience within religious systems. And yet, these intersections also hold the key to understanding the depth of that harm and the paths we can take to heal from it.

When you're in the middle of it, it's so hard to see. The systems feel so big, the teachings so ingrained, and the weight of it all feels like it's just part of who you are. You're taught to carry it without question, to see it as normal, as righteous, even as love. But when you start to untangle the harm, you see it for what it really is: a framework that wasn't built to include or affirm everyone. A system that teaches conditional worth instead of unconditional love. And when you finally see it, there's no unseeing it.

The stories in this chapter aren't just about pain. They're about survival. They're about people who have held onto pieces of themselves, even when everything around them tried to strip those pieces away. They're about the courage it takes to speak up, to ask for more, to believe you deserve better. And they're about the hope that comes from reclaiming what was lost. From saying, "I am enough, just as I am."

If we want to move forward, if we want to create spaces where healing is possible, we have to start here. We have to listen to the people who have been left out, dismissed, or told they didn't belong. Not to argue or defend the system but to truly listen. Because their stories hold the truths we need to hear. And if we're willing to sit with those truths without judgment, we might just learn something that changes everything.

Healing isn't about fixing ourselves; it's about letting go of the idea that we were broken in the first place. It's about making space for every part of who we are and letting that be enough. And it's about creating something better, together. A world where all of us, in all our complexities, can feel seen, valued, and whole.

Reflection:

What parts of your identity shaped how you were seen or unseen inside your faith community?

What parts do you struggle to see in others?

Reminder:

You are allowed to be all of who you are.

You are allowed to hold all of your story, even the parts others tried to erase.

Chapter 7

When Leaving Breaks You

The Grief and Cost of Walking Away

S he was the kind of member I was taught I should be.

She prayed every morning, waking up early to read her scriptures before her kids woke up, underlining verses with color-coded markers, and jotting impressions in the margins. Her Sunday School lessons were planned two weeks early, not just because she wanted to be prepared but because she wanted to study deeply. Line upon line. With commentary. With prayer.

She brought meals when someone was sick. Babysat for temple nights. Bore her testimony even when her voice trembled.

She was the one they called when a Relief Society sister was struggling or when the missionaries needed someone to bring a new investigator to church. She didn't drink soda. Didn't watch R-rated movies. She fasted with reverence.

Her patriarchal blessing was memorized. Her garments were worn without complaint, even in the heat of summer. She believed.

And when she knelt down, really knelt, she wasn't just hoping for an answer. She expected it. That's what she had always been taught. Ask in faith, never wavering. If you study religiously, if you pray with real intent, the Spirit will tell you what's right.

So when it came, quiet but unmistakable, she couldn't unknow it.

It didn't come with thunder or fear. It came with clarity. She was sitting in the temple, staring at the veil, when something shifted. A knowing dropped into her body, something deeper than logic, more certain than doubt.

This isn't truth anymore.

That was all. No anger. No rebellion. Just clarity.

She shook it off at first. Went home and fasted again. Read her scriptures harder. Went to the bishop. But it wouldn't go away. The answer she got, the one she was promised would come if she was faithful, had arrived. And it was not what she was supposed to feel.

This is what they never warned you about. That sometimes the revelation takes you away from the very system that taught you to listen. That sometimes, doing everything "right" doesn't lead you deeper into the faith. It leads you out of it.

And that's when the real unraveling begins.

But not everyone leaves.

Many people choose to stay. Some find ways to carve out a livable space inside their faith tradition. Others don't get to choose. They're pushed out, released from callings without explanation, quietly excluded, or formally excommunicated. Cut off from their community and their eternal covenants in one official sweep.

Some walk away gently after years of trying to stay. Others flee after one breaking point too many. And some wake up one day and just know, with a clarity that cannot be unknown.

This chapter isn't about deciding whether to stay or leave. It's about the grief and confusion and trauma that can follow when you do leave. Whatever led you there, choice, whether revelation, betrayal, or rejection, this part of the story matters too.

Because leaving doesn't always feel like freedom.

Sometimes it feels like collapse.

Loss of Belonging

For many, leaving religion doesn't start with liberation. It starts with loneliness.

The community that once held you no longer feels safe or you're no longer welcome. The rhythm of Sundays disappears. Holidays lose their shape. Language changes. Inside jokes don't land anymore. Even the cadence of prayer or the smell of the chapel carpet can leave your body aching for what you no longer have access to.

It's more than missing people. It's a rupture from a whole system of belonging. A way of seeing the world. A shared set of meanings, phrases, and answers to unanswerable questions. The people who once celebrated your milestones, baptisms, missions, and sealings may now silently grieve your decisions or speak of you with pity. Some step away with quiet sorrow. Others pull away with force. They may never say the words, but the message is clear: you are not one of us anymore.

And sometimes, the loss is not just external. It's inside you.

Even if you're surrounded by new support, there can still be a profound ache for what once was. Belonging isn't something we just know. It's something we feel. And for those raised in systems like the LDS Church, belonging was never a casual thing. It was eternal. It was wrapped into covenants, identity, and salvation. It wasn't just about being part of a group. It was about being sealed to your family forever, about being counted among the righteous, about knowing exactly where you stood.

Leaving that behind can feel like choosing disconnection. Even when you know it's the right thing. Even when your body says it's safe to walk away. The longing to belong doesn't disappear. It just has nowhere to go.

And that ache, that emptiness, can be deeply disorienting. Especially when it's coupled with shame. Because the story many of us were told is that if we ever left, we'd feel lost. And then, when we do feel lost, it feels like they were right. But what that story fails to name is, of course, you feel lost. You were taught that the only place you could ever feel found, feel happiness, was inside the system you just left.

That's not failure. That's trauma.

Internalized Fear and Conditioning

The fear doesn't leave just because you stopped believing.

Even when the theology starts to unravel. Even when you know, deep in your body, that you don't belong there anymore. The fear stays. Quiet at first. Subtle. But constant. It lives in the moments you don't expect. When you hear a hymn at the grocery store. When you pass the temple and your chest tightens. When someone asks what ward you're in and you freeze, not because you don't have an answer but because your answer feels like a confession.

It is fear, yes. But underneath the fear is something even heavier. Shame.

We were taught to be afraid of getting it wrong. But more than that, we were taught to believe that we were the problem. That doubt meant we lacked faith. That discomfort meant we had wandered. That if the Spirit was gone, it was because we had done something to drive it away.

So we tried harder. We prayed more. We fasted. We searched our hearts. We begged for peace. And when it still didn't feel right, we assumed we had failed. That we weren't faithful enough. That we weren't clean enough. That we didn't deserve the clarity we were seeking.

And then we left.

But leaving didn't feel like freedom. Not right away. It felt like crossing a line we had been warned about our whole lives. It felt like walking away from being good.

That is where the shame lives.

It rises in your chest when you hear someone say "families are forever." It coils in your stomach when your child asks about heaven. It grips your throat when someone you love bears their testimony, and you wonder if they're praying for you. Even when you are sure of your choice, that voice still lingers. Maybe you were deceived. Maybe you weren't strong enough to stay. Maybe this pain is exactly what you were warned about.

And that's what makes it so hard to name. The shame doesn't shout. It whispers. It speaks in the language we were raised on. It sounds like obedience. It feels like humility. It moves through our bodies in ways that feel familiar and sacred.

But it isn't sacred. It is internalized control. It is trauma, misnamed as truth.

Some wonder, "What if I made the wrong choice?" But more often, it goes further. "What if I am ruining this for everyone else?" "What if my leaving is the reason my kids don't believe?" "What if I hurt my parents beyond repair?" "What if I broke something eternal?" That isn't just fear. That is shame, layered with responsibility, speaking in the voice of God.

Cognitive Dissonance and Identity Crisis

It doesn't unravel all at once. It starts with one thread.

A teaching that suddenly feels off. A moment in church when your body tenses before your brain can explain why. A conference talk that once brought comfort but now leaves you unsettled. You tell yourself it's just a phase. You double down on scripture study. You go to the temple more often. You pray harder. And for a while, that works.

Until it doesn't.

Until the thread pulls a little further and another belief comes loose. Then another. You start to realize that the answers that once felt so sure are no longer enough. That what you're told to feel and what you *actually* feel are no longer matching. The dissonance builds slowly at first, then all at once.

And it is dizzying.

Because you were taught to see the world in a very specific way. There was a plan. A purpose. A clear line between truth and deception. And now, without warning, that clarity is gone. What you were certain of yesterday is crumbling beneath you. And with it goes the scaffolding of your identity.

One woman I interviewed described sitting in a temple recommend interview, answering the questions just as she always had. But when she said yes to believing having a testimony about the restoration of the LDS Church, a question about believing in Joseph Smith, her voice caught. Her hands went cold. Her chest tightened for just a moment. She couldn't explain why. Nothing had changed in her answers. But something had changed in her body. Later she told me, "I didn't stop believing. I just didn't know how to answer anymore." And that was the moment it started to fall apart. Not all at once but piece by piece.

Who are you if you are not a daughter of God?

Who are you if you are no longer preparing for exaltation?

Who are you if you no longer know what comes after this life?

These aren't just theological questions. They are identity fractures. Everything was built on one foundation. Your choices, your relationships, your understanding of love, sacrifice, and eternity. You were taught to trust it. To build your life on it. To sing of its strength and never question its cracks. But when that foundation starts to crumble, it doesn't just shake your beliefs. It shakes your sense of self. It does not leave you standing. It leaves you hollow. Like a house built on sand or someone else's promise. And in the quiet that follows, you are left asking what still belongs to you. What is real. What you want to rebuild. And what was never yours to begin with.

Some try to hold both realities. To stay and shift. To believe and question at the same time. But the weight of that internal tension is exhausting. It's the quiet panic of saying one thing while feeling another. The ache of being surrounded by people who still believe when you no longer can. The heartbreak of wondering if there's something wrong with you for not being able to make it fit anymore.

And for many, that in-between becomes unbearable.

You don't just lose your faith. You lose your bearings. You lose your language. You lose the version of yourself you were always supposed to become.

That is not just confusion. That is grief. That is collapse.

And that collapse is a trauma in and of itself. Because when you were never taught how to live outside the system, stepping into the unknown doesn't feel brave. It feels like being lost.

Why People Stay

Not everyone leaves.

Some people live for years in that in-between space, holding both faith and doubt in the same breath. Others find a way to stay that doesn't require full belief, adjusting the terms of their belonging quietly, without ever needing to say it out loud. And some never question at all. Or if they do, it doesn't lead them out. The reasons people stay are not simple. They are layered, personal, and deeply human.

Some stay because it's home. Because it's where their memories live. Their family, their traditions, and their community. It's the place that raised them. The people who showed up with casseroles after surgeries and stood beside them in every milestone. For many, leaving would mean walking away from everything that once made them feel safe, even if that safety now feels complicated.

Others stay because they still believe. Not just in the rules or the doctrine but in the feeling. The Spirit. The prayers that brought them peace in dark seasons. The rituals that helped them make meaning. Even when parts of the system hurt, they still find goodness in the heart of it. That kind of belief isn't shallow. It's sacred. And it holds a deep kind of weight that isn't easily let go of.

Some stay because it's all they've ever known. The church has been their nervous system, their framework for reality, their source of emotional regulation. It taught them how to make choices, how to show up, how to be good. Without it, life feels unstructured. Untethered. Staying doesn't mean they aren't aware of the harm. Sometimes, staying is the only way they know how to survive.

Others stay because leaving would cost too much. Their partner isn't ready. Their children are still growing up inside it. Their job, housing, and emotional support is all intertwined with the faith community. They aren't choosing to stay out of fear. They're choosing to stay because they are already stretched thin and don't have the capacity to lose one more thing.

And some stay because they've never seen another way. When you're raised believing this is the one true path, the only safe place, the only real source of happiness or hope, stepping away doesn't just feel scary, it feels impossible. Not because they're weak. Because the story they were told didn't leave space for anything else.

So no, staying doesn't mean someone is unaware or unwilling to grow. Sometimes, staying is an act of strength. Sometimes, it is protection.

Sometimes, it is a way to preserve something sacred in a system that doesn't always feel safe.

And for those who stay, that choice can come with its own kind of pain. The pain of silence. The pain of knowing. The pain of continuing to show up in a space that has harmed you or the people you love. That complexity matters too. Because you don't have to leave to feel the weight of what this system has taken. You just have to be honest enough to name it.

This book is not a judgment of anyone's religious beliefs or spiritual practices. It is a witness to the pain of religious trauma experienced by those within religion. The ones who stayed. The ones who left. The ones in between. The ones who hold both harm and meaning in the same breath.

The Guilt of Hurting Others

And still, for those who do leave, one of the hardest parts is knowing it doesn't just impact you.

You can make peace with your decision. You can trust it deep in your body. You can feel more whole and more honest than you ever have. And still, there can be a grief so sharp it steals your breath because you know this is hurting the people you love.

You were taught that your choices ripple outward. That your righteousness strengthens others. That your rebellion leads them astray. You were taught that families are eternal but only if you all stay worthy.

So when you step outside that path, even quietly, even with love, it can feel like you're tearing something sacred apart.

I've sat with so many people who've said, "I know this is right for me, but I still feel like I've ruined it for everyone else." They worry they've disappointed their parents. That they're breaking their children's chances at eternal life. That their partner will never see them the same. That their siblings are praying for them in quiet desperation. That their name is now a whispered concern in a testimony meeting.

It doesn't matter that the theology no longer feels true. The guilt still clings. Because it was never just about beliefs. It was about love. And when love was framed as obedience, choosing something different starts to feel like betrayal.

So they carry that weight. They soften their truth. They let themselves become the problem so their loved ones don't have to sit with the loss. They show up to baptisms and sealings with a tight smile and an aching chest. They try to explain themselves without making anyone else uncomfortable. They say, "I still believe in God" before anyone asks, just to reassure them. They say, "I'm okay" when they aren't.

Because it's easier to carry the guilt than to watch someone else's heart break.

But guilt isn't the same as harm. You are allowed to choose what is true for you. You are allowed to leave without taking responsibility for other people's discomfort. You are allowed to love people without following their rules. You are allowed to walk away without needing to be the villain in someone else's story.

The grief of hurting people doesn't mean you did something wrong. It means you were part of a system where love and compliance were fused so tightly that choosing yourself was never part of the equation.

Until now.

Relational Breakdown

You expect the doctrine to be hard to let go of. You expect the grief. You expect the shame. But what often cuts the deepest is what happens to your relationships.

People pull away.

Sometimes it's immediate, a calling released, a friend who stops answering your texts, a bishop who avoids eye contact in the grocery store. Other times it's subtle. The conversations shrink. The invitations stop coming. You are still loved but at a distance. Like something about you is now unsafe to be around.

And it hurts. Not just because of what is lost but because these were the people who knew you best. The ones you shared years of connection with. The ones you served with. The ones who sat beside you in Relief Society, brought meals after surgery, included your kids in every activity, and always said yes to your name on the prayer roll. And now, without much warning, you've become someone they don't know how to talk to.

One woman I interviewed had been in the same ward for more than fifteen years. She had raised her kids there. She was the one who dropped off freezer meals, sent check-in texts, and showed up when someone's husband was hospitalized. She had held babies in the mother's lounge while other women cried in the hallway. She knew birthdays, anniversaries, and who liked lemon bars instead of brownies.

And when she left the Church, it went silent.

No one reached out. Not a single message. No one asked how she was. No one asked why. Except one friend, who came over twice in the first few months just to sit and listen. The third time she came, she brought a conference talk and asked her to come back. It wasn't cruel. But it wasn't connection anymore.

Her name was never mentioned to her again. But it showed up on the list. The "not currently active, how do we bring them back" list. The one passed around in ward council. The one where you become a task instead of a person.

For many, the pain isn't just that the relationship changed. It's how quickly it changed. One honest conversation. One decision to stop attending. One quiet step away. And suddenly, the love feels thinner. The interactions disappear. The ward becomes something you have to recover from instead of something you grieve.

Some families close ranks. Some friendships vanish entirely. Some marriages strain under the weight of trying to hold two opposing worlds in one home. There are people who choose to stay in the relationship but never fully stay open. And there are people who walk away, convinced that your loss of faith is a betrayal they can't recover from.

It is a kind of heartbreak that doesn't come with closure. Because nothing dramatic happened. You didn't stop loving them. You just stopped believing. And that was enough to break something.

The system never taught us how to love unconditionally. It taught us how to love righteously. Which means many of the relationships we built were shaped by performance, shared belief, shared obedience, and shared eternal goals. So when you leave, it doesn't just feel like you've changed. It feels like you've broken the agreement.

But you didn't. The agreement was conditional. You just finally stopped pretending it wasn't.

The Body's Response

Sometimes the body is the last one to let go. And sometimes, it's the first to know.

Long before the decision is made, your body might already be bracing. You sit in sacrament meeting and feel a wave of nausea. You walk into the temple and your chest tightens. You hear someone bear testimony, and your throat closes, even as you smile. These are not signs of rebellion. They're signs of dissonance. Your body is speaking what you haven't yet found the words to say.

And then, at some point, maybe immediately, maybe years later, your body crashes.

For some, it happens as soon as they step away. For others, it doesn't come until much later, when the urgency has faded, when they've built a new life and feel mostly okay. That's often when the body finally starts to speak. When the system is no longer surviving, it starts to feel. When the fight to hold it all together softens, the collapse comes. Not as a setback but as a release. A sign that something in you finally believes it's safe enough now to fall apart.

Sometimes, it looks like exhaustion. Not just tiredness but the kind of fatigue that makes your bones ache. Other times, it shows up as anxiety, panic, or numbness. For some, it comes through physical illness, tight muscles, migraines, or flare-ups that don't make sense. And for many, it's emotional. A sudden surge of sadness. Rage that was buried under obedience. A grief that was too big to hold at the time.

None of it is random. The body has been holding this for years. Holding your silence. Holding your vigilance. Holding the pressure to be worthy, to be good, to be safe. And once the system begins to trust that it doesn't have to hold that anymore, it lets go. Not because something is wrong but because something is finally ready.

But letting go doesn't always feel peaceful. It often feels like collapse.

Because the nervous system has been functioning in survival mode. For some, since childhood. Obedience became regulation. Certainty became safe. And when that structure is gone, whether you're still grieving or you've already rebuilt, your body may suddenly feel unmoored.

People say, "I thought I would feel free." And maybe that comes. But for many, first comes collapse. Then disorientation. Then, eventually, if we keep listening, a new kind of grounding.

This is the body doing what it was never allowed to do before. Not breaking. Not failing. Just finally, finally letting itself feel.

Leaving Doesn't Always Feel Like Freedom

There's a story people like to tell about those who leave religion. That they were offended. That they wanted to sin. That they didn't try hard enough. That they're angry and bitter and can't let it go.

But that's not the story I hear.

The story I hear is one of heartbreak. Of people who stayed for as long as they could. Who prayed. Who tried. Who gave everything they had. The story I hear is full of silence. Years of not speaking the truth out loud. Years of performing belief while holding grief just below the surface. Years of hoping something would shift. That something would make it okay to stay.

And then one day it isn't okay anymore. And you leave.

And you expect freedom. Or at least relief. But what often comes first is collapse. Grief. Disorientation. A deep sense of loss. You lose your community. Your map. Your identity. Sometimes your family. Sometimes your marriage. Sometimes your ability to recognize yourself.

And no one tells you how to hold that.

No one tells you that leaving doesn't always feel empowering. Sometimes, it feels like falling. Like being completely alone. Like starting over without any tools or language or familiar ground.

And that doesn't mean you made the wrong choice.

It means you left a system that trained you to believe it was the only way to be whole. It means your body and your mind are trying to find their footing outside of something that once defined everything. It means your nervous system is catching up to the truth your spirit already knew.

There is trauma in staying too long.

And there is trauma in walking away.

Both can be true.

And neither is the end of the story.

This is where the real work begins.

Reflection:

What did you lose when you walked away or when you stayed?
What, even now, do you still grieve?

Reminder:

You were never wrong for needing more.
You were never wrong for wanting to belong to yourself.

Part 3

Becoming Me

Finesse Literary Press Ltd.

Chapter 8

Reclaiming What Was Taken

Tools for Healing the Self

*H*ealing isn't about finding the right answer. It's about finally asking your own questions.

Religious trauma runs deep because it shapes the very foundation of how we understand ourselves, our worth, our safety, and our choices. When that foundation cracks or falls away, what's left can feel like chaos. But that chaos is the beginning. It's the start of finding you again.

This chapter isn't a checklist. These tools are here for you to try on. To be curious. To explore. For those doing the work of healing and the professionals walking alongside them.

Her name was Claire.

When she came to me, she wasn't angry. She wasn't sad. She wasn't even sure what she was feeling. She wasn't just tired. She was worn out from the inside out, like she had been carrying too much for too long.

Claire had spent her whole life doing everything right. She was the good student. The good wife. The good mother. The one who showed up. The one who said yes. The one who kept it all moving.

At home, she carried the invisible weight of everything. The parenting. The household. The emotional labor. She managed it all, believing that if she did it well enough, if she stayed good enough, everything would be okay.

But it wasn't. The responsibilities kept growing. Her partner wasn't helping. The cracks in the relationship widened. And when she reached out, when she tried to name what she needed, she was told she was too much. Too emotional. Too sensitive.

It was her fault.If she was struggling, it was because she wasn't trying hard enough.If she needed help, it was because she was asking for too much.

So she tried harder. She gave more. She disappeared a little more every day.

And still, it wasn't enough.

She sat across from me, hands clenched together, eyes filled with quiet panic, and said, "I keep doing everything I can. Everything I'm supposed to. And somehow it's still my fault. I still feel like I'm failing."

She didn't use the language of earned worth. She didn't talk about how deeply she had been taught that her value came from service, sacrifice, and silence. She only knew the ache of it. The exhaustion. The shame. The desperate hope that if she just did a little more, if she was just a little better, she would finally be enough.

But no amount of doing could make her feel worthy. Because the system she was living in, the rules she had been taught, were never built to make her whole. They were built to keep her striving.

The work ahead of her, the work ahead of so many of us, wasn't about doing more. It was about breaking the spell of earned worth. It was about beginning, for the first time, to listen for her own voice underneath all the noise. The voice that had been there all along. The voice that already knew:

You are enough. You have always been enough.

Understanding Where Beliefs Begin

Core beliefs are quiet truths that live inside us. Not your religious or spiritual beliefs but the things you've internalized about who you are and how you're supposed to show up in the world. These usually don't come from one moment. They build over time. In patterns. In glances. In expectations. In silence. And eventually, your system starts to treat them like the truth. They become the verbalizations of a one thousand small wounds from religious trauma.

Most of these beliefs go back further than we realize. They start before language, sometimes in the preverbal years. Others are generational, passed down through looks, tones, and unspoken lessons. We learn them from how the people around us act and treat themselves, from the primary songs we sing and the expectations woven into religious teachings. What gets reinforced over time is not just the belief itself but the shame that comes with it. The shame of being too much. Not enough. Too loud. Too sensitive. Too curious. These early messages become the wiring, the way we learn what love feels like, what safety looks like, and which parts of us are allowed to exist.

That's why this part of the work matters. It's not just about what you believe now. It's about understanding what you learned, how you made sense of the world at each stage of development, and how those perceptions became embedded. They show up everywhere. In your parenting, your work, and your body. In how you define worth and love. And until we bring them into awareness, we keep living by them without even realizing it.

Claire didn't wake up one day believing she wasn't enough. It happened slowly, through years of small moments, quiet lessons, and impossible expectations that became her truth.

Identifying Internalized Beliefs

You usually don't start by knowing the belief. You start by noticing the tension. The guilt when you say no. The fear that you did something wrong. The exhaustion that doesn't go away, no matter how much you get done. Or maybe it's the inner critic, the voice inside your head judging and shaming everything you do. These moments are clues.

They point to something deeper running underneath: an internalized rule your system is still trying to follow.

The work is learning how to trace that feeling back. To pause and ask: *what would I have to believe to feel this way right now?* And then: *where did I learn that?* Sometimes, it's clear. Sometimes, it takes time. These beliefs often live just under the surface, shaping how you speak to yourself and how you move through the world. But once you name one, even just one, something starts to shift.

Here are some of the most common internalized beliefs that show up in people recovering from religious trauma:

- *I am not enough.*

- *I have to be perfect to be good.*

- *I can't trust myself.*

- *My worth is in how much I give.*

- *My body is dangerous.*

- *Sex is shameful. My body is shameful.*

- *If I obey, I will be loved.*

- *I will be holy if I suffer.*

- *Joy is selfish.*

- *If I question, I will be punished.*

- *I am responsible for other people's feelings and salvation.*

- *Doubt is sin.*

- *Anger means I'm unrighteous.*

- *Belonging only comes if I hide parts of myself.*

- *God is watching and is disappointed.*

The most common version I see in women sounds something like this: **I have to be _____ in order to be loved, to have worth, or to truly belong.**

Everyone fills in that blank a little differently. I have to be good. I have to be quiet. I have to be strong. I have to be pure. I have to be needed. I have to be less.

Whatever the belief is, it often lives just beneath awareness. Not always as a conscious thought but in how you speak to yourself, how you make decisions, and how you show up in relationships. In the next section, we'll begin to explore how to separate those beliefs from your truth. This isn't just about healing what was. It's about reclaiming the life you are living now.

And it's important to say this clearly. This isn't about blaming where the belief came from. Trauma and belief systems are shaped by perception and how we experienced the world at whatever stage we were in. That's where we start. Not just with the belief you hold now but with what it meant when you first felt it.

Most of the time, when we trace it back, we find familiar beliefs: *I have to be good to be loved. I have to be selfless to belong. I have to be strong to be worthy.* These aren't just thoughts. They're survival strategies. And they were never actually yours. They were taught. Conditioned. Expected. You get to start hearing them now. You get to question them. Not because you failed but because you're finally safe enough to ask where they came from.

***

Try This:

Start with a Sentence

What's one sentence that comes up often in your head, especially in moments of stress, shame, or fear? Write it down. Then ask:

- What do I have to believe for this to feel true?

- Where might I have learned that?

- How old was I when I started to learn it?

Trace It Back

Pick a belief you hold now, like "I'm not enough" or "I have to get it right."

Ask:

- What does this belief expect of me?

- What part of me is still trying to earn love or belonging?

- Can I remember when I first felt this, even if I didn't have words for it?

Try a Reframe

Take that belief and shift it gently. Not into toxic positivity but into compassion.

- "I'm a burden" → "I was never too much. I just needed care."

- "I have to be good" → "I don't have to earn love. I already deserve it."

***

Tip From a Therapist: "Not Enough" Isn't your actual core belief

After working with hundreds of women and hundreds more therapists across all spectrums of belief, from devout to deconstructed, there's one phrase I hear more than almost anything else:

"I'm not good enough."
Not a good enough mom.
Not a good enough wife.
Not a good enough woman.
Not a good enough caretaker.
Not a good enough friend.
Not a good enough anything.

But here's what I've come to understand. That statement, *"I'm not enough,"* isn't the real belief. It's the language of shame. It's the way we learned to speak our pain in a way society would tolerate. It doesn't disrupt the system. It doesn't challenge the rules. It fits.

Because we were taught that worth isn't inherent. It has to be earned. Through goodness. Through service. Through getting it all right.

So when someone says they feel like they're not enough, it's not about failure. It's about fear, fear that they won't be loved, belong, or be safe unless they keep proving themselves. Over and over. Without rest.

When we slow it down, when we trace the thread, we find the deeper belief hiding underneath:

- "I have to take care of everyone around me to be worthy."

- "If I'm not giving everything, I don't deserve love."

- "If I drop the ball, I disappear."

That's where the real work begins. Not in trying to fix the shame but in learning to hear what it's trying to protect.

***

Emotional Intelligence and Regulation

You were taught to manage your behavior. Now, you get to feel your emotions.

Many of us were never taught how to do emotion. Instead, we learned how to hide it, how to perform over it, how to be good, calm, and grateful. We weren't shown how to feel sad, mad, or scared. We learned how to shut those feelings down quickly, quietly, before anyone noticed.

People rarely come into therapy saying, "I need to work on my emotions." They say, "I'm overwhelmed," or "I'm anxious all the time," or "I feel numb and disconnected, and I don't understand why." When we begin to slow things down, we usually find emotions were never safe in the first place. They weren't modeled, named, or welcomed.

It's not just that we didn't learn how to feel; it's that the way we learned not to feel created deep belief systems, beliefs like: "If I feel this, I'll fall apart." "If I get angry, I'll hurt someone." "If I cry, it means I'm weak." "If I feel too much, I'll be too much." These beliefs embed themselves deeply, and we shape our lives around avoiding what we were never allowed to experience.

But here's what we know now: Emotion is not just a feeling. It's a full-body experience rooted in biology, shaped by meaning, and woven through every relationship we have. Emotions aren't problems to fix; they're messages meant to guide us. Fear protects us. Anger defends us. Sadness helps us slow down and heal. Joy connects us.

We often fear or silence certain emotions, categorizing them into good or bad, but emotions were never meant to be divided that way. They're part of how we survive, belong, and understand our world. When emotions are allowed to move freely, they rise and fall naturally, like waves. When suppressed, they harden into anxiety, numbness, and disconnection. Emotion itself was never the issue. Losing our ability to feel was.

When we talk about emotional intelligence, we aren't referring to becoming hyper self-aware or having perfect words. We're talking about building a new relationship with our emotions and learning to allow all of our feelings. It's about staying present with ourselves through anger, sadness, and grief and resisting the urge to shut it all down prematurely.

This part of the work can feel messy, even wrong. Your body might resist at first, and that's okay. It doesn't mean you're doing it incorrectly. It means you're finally beginning to feel what's real. And feeling what's real is the start of genuine healing.

Turning off your emotions has a cost. Claire had spent so long carrying everything, keeping herself small and silent, that she stopped knowing what she felt at all. She didn't come into therapy talking about anger, or sadness, or fear. She came in overwhelmed. Exhausted.

Numb. She had learned early that emotions were good or bad. That some were of the Holy Spirit, divine, and some were of the devil, wrong. She learned that anger was bad. That sadness was weakness. That needing too much made you selfish. So she stayed quiet. She stayed grateful. She stayed small.

But even as she kept trying, the cracks kept widening. The boundaries she tried to set were ignored. The help she asked for never came. And somewhere underneath, the numbness and anger started to rise. It terrified her. It had been buried so long she didn't know what to do with it. It felt like it would be too much, big, dangerous, and shameful. At first, she would catch herself feeling it, a flash of frustration, a moment of resentment, and shut it down before it could breathe. "I shouldn't feel this way," she would say. "I should just be grateful."

But the anger was real. It was the part of her that knew her worth was being violated. It was the part of her that still believed she deserved to be seen. Learning to feel her anger wasn't graceful. It was messy, tender, and slow. But every time she allowed herself to feel it, even a little, something inside her shifted. She started reclaiming parts of herself she had been taught to hide. And behind the anger, once it was safe enough, came the grief. Not the tidy grief people expect but the real grief. The grief of years spent carrying what wasn't hers. The grief of being invisible even when she did everything right. The grief of all the parts of herself she had abandoned just to survive.

Feeling her emotions didn't make Claire selfish. It made her real. It made her whole. But learning to feel her emotions also uncovered something harder. Claire had built her life around taking care of everyone else: her children, her partner, and her community. She loved them fiercely. She showed up every day with everything she had. And somewhere along the way, she slowly disappeared.

Motherhood had become everything. Not because she regretted it, not because she didn't love her children, but because somewhere deep down, she had learned that her worth lived in how well she served, how much she gave, and how little she asked for herself. She didn't know how to take care of herself. She didn't know what she liked or what she wanted. She didn't know who she was outside of the responsibilities she carried.

When I asked her what she did just for herself, she sat in silence. When I asked her what made her feel alive, she didn't have an answer. Anger had cracked the door open. Grief had started to show up. And now, standing in the quiet wreckage of survival, the hardest question was waiting: if I am not only what I give to others, then who am I?

Claire didn't have the answer yet. But she was finally allowed to ask the question. And that, too, was part of coming home to herself.

Learning to feel again doesn't give you clarity overnight. But it starts to make room. For your anger. For your grief. For your truth. And in that space, you begin to heal and to rebuild.

***

Try This:

Learning How to Do Emotion

You don't have to get it perfect. You don't even have to know what you're feeling right away. The goal here is just to get familiar. To give yourself a little space to notice what's happening underneath the surface without shutting it down.

Start with your body
When something feels off, and you're overwhelmed, frustrated, shut down, whatever it is, pause for a moment. Drop into your body.

Ask:

- *Where do I feel this?*

- *What does it feel like? Is it tight? Heavy? Buzzy? Numb?*
  You don't have to explain it. Just notice it's there.

See if it has a name
Try putting a word to the feeling. Not a perfect word, just something close. Sad. Angry. Lonely. Hopeful.
If you've spent years avoiding your emotions, this part might feel frustrating. That's okay. You're not doing it wrong. You're learning a language you were never taught. Start simple.

Let it be there, just for a minute
Set a timer for sixty seconds. That's how long most emotions take to move through your system when you don't block them.

Breathe. Let the feeling exist. You don't have to fix it or do anything with it. Just stay with it and remind yourself, *I can feel this and still be okay.*

Ask what it's trying to tell you.

After the wave passes, gently ask:

- *What was that feeling trying to say?*

- *What did it need from me?*
  You don't need a clear answer. The asking is the practice.

***

Tip From a Therapist: Emotions Are Just Information

Emotions are often just information. They're not always big or over-whelming; sometimes, they're subtle signals your system is picking up on. They're shaped by your past, your body, your nervous system, and your relationships. They're not random, and they're definitely not wrong.

But when religious trauma is in the mix, emotions often get filtered through a lens of morality. You were taught some feelings were good, and others were bad. Some were signs of righteousness. Others were selfish or sinful. So when those old teachings get triggered, you might find yourself thinking, *"This feeling is bad,"* or *"I shouldn't feel this way.*" That's not true. That's conditioning. That's your trauma coming online to protect you, trying to shut the emotions down.

It's not your fault. But it might be keeping you stuck.

When you begin to sit with your emotions, even for a few moments, you start to widen your emotional tolerance. Once you've done that a few times, try asking yourself: *And what else am I feeling?* Because most of us don't feel one thing at a time. We feel grief and anger. Guilt and sadness. Hope and fear. Those feelings can overlap and even contradict each other, which makes everything feel more intense than it really is.

If this part feels especially hard, go back to the beliefs. Ask: *What do I believe about feeling this? What was I taught about what it says about me? What did I learn happens when people feel this way?* Because often, what keeps us stuck isn't the feeling itself, it's the meaning we've attached to it.

***

Identity Work

You don't have to know who you are to begin. But you do have to start asking.

When you've spent your whole life being told who to be, what to believe, what's right, what's wrong, how to show up, and what makes you worthy. Identity is shaped around survival, not self. You learn how to become the version of yourself that keeps you safe. The version who fits the mold. The one who doesn't question too much and earns belonging by following the rules.

But eventually, something doesn't fit anymore. You start saying no when you used to say yes. You feel anger when you're told to be grateful. You want things you were never allowed to want. And suddenly, the version of you that kept everything together starts to fall apart. You're left wondering, *If I'm not that, then who am I?*

That's not a crisis. That's the beginning.

Identity work rarely starts with clarity. It usually starts with grief, the grief of realizing you don't know what's actually yours. You've been living by someone else's blueprint, someone else's expectations. What you believed, what you wanted, what you needed to do to be loved, so much of it was handed to you. And now that you're ready to question it, it can feel terrifying. Because when you stop being who they needed you to be, it might feel like you're risking everything.

And, in many ways, you are.

You might lose relationships. You might lose certainty. You might lose the comfort of knowing exactly what to do to be accepted.

But identity isn't something you figure out and then lock in. It's not a final product. It's a relationship you build over time. It's about returning to yourself, again and again, as you grow and shift and heal.

It doesn't show up in one big moment. It shows up in layers, in small choices. A decision that feels a little more honest. A shirt you stop wearing because it was never really you. A way your body moves when no one's watching and how it softens when it's not being judged.

Identity is not a destination. It's something you notice and nurture and grow into with space, permission, and curiosity. You don't need a label or a perfect understanding to begin. You just need to ask a different question than the ones you were given. And then notice what answers come up.

***

Try This:

A Small Truth

When you've spent your life being told who you are and how to act, it can be hard to know who you are. You were shaped by rules, by expectations, by the constant message of what was acceptable and what wasn't. You became what was needed. What was safe. What was praised.

So identity work doesn't start with clarity. It starts with noticing. With friction. With that gut feeling that something doesn't feel true anymore, even if you don't have the words for why.

Start here. Gently.

Take a moment and ask yourself:

- Where am I saying yes when I really want to say no or not today?

- Where am I doing something out of habit, not choice?

- What part of me disappears around certain people?

- Where do I feel most disconnected from myself?

- What parts of me only show up when I'm alone?

You don't have to fix anything right now. You don't even have to understand it yet. Just notice what's coming up.

Then try one small truth. Say no when you usually say yes. Wear the thing that feels a little risky. Take a breath before you respond. Be honest, even if it's quiet.

It doesn't have to be dramatic. It just has to be real.

Doing something new, especially when you've spent your life following rules, will feel unfamiliar. It might make other people uncomfortable. You'll feel that discomfort in your body. That doesn't mean you're doing it wrong. It means you're doing something different. And that discomfort fades with time, practice, and self-trust.

After, check in with yourself:

- How did that feel?

- Did I feel more like myself, even for a moment?

- What did I notice in my body?

- Would I do that again? Would I shift anything next time?

That's it. That's how identity starts to rebuild, not by reinventing yourself all at once but by letting yourself be a little more honest than you were before. One small truth at a time.

And if today isn't the day? That's okay. You can try again next week. Or next year. You don't have to become someone else. You just get to stop being who you were never given a choice about.

***

Tip From a Therapist: The Fear Underneath Identity Work

Not knowing who you are can feel terrifying. But it's not just about identity. It's about uncertainty. When your sense of self has been shaped by roles and rules, certainty becomes survival. Knowing what's expected. What's right. How to belong. It gives you control in a world where control often felt like the only safety you had.

So when you start letting go of that, even just a little, your nervous system might panic. Not because you're doing it wrong but because the unknown used to be dangerous. In so many religious systems, not knowing was framed as weakness. As failure. As rebellion.

That's why identity work often stirs fear. Fear of making the wrong choice. Fear of becoming someone who's no longer accepted. Fear of stepping outside the box and not being able to find your way back.

But here's the truth. This process isn't about getting it right. It's about trying things on. The way a teenager stands in front of a mirror experimenting. You try something. See how it feels. Take it off. Try again. You ask, Did I like that? Did it feel like me? Was there a part that did? A part that didn't?

You're not locking anything in. You're learning. You're exploring from the version of you that exists today, not the one who had to survive yesterday.

And something that doesn't feel true now might feel completely different in three years. That doesn't mean you were wrong before. It means you've grown.

That's what identity work really is. Curiosity. Trying. Noticing. Choosing. And allowing yourself to evolve, without needing to explain it to anyone, not even yourself.

***

For Claire, learning to feel her emotions was only the beginning.

As the anger surfaced, so did the sorrow. The deeper she went, the more she began to see not just what had been taken from her but what had never been given in the first place. The freedom to be whole. The right to belong without conditions. The life she might have lived if she hadn't spent so many years trying to be good enough.

That's where grief begins for so many of us. Not in what we lost all at once but in what was never fully allowed to exist.

It's not just about mourning what happened. It's about grieving the space that was never made for your full self. The questions you were never allowed to ask. The choices you were never given. The parts of you that had to stay hidden just to feel safe.

And slowly, piece by piece, that grief clears a path. It softens the ground. It makes room for something new.

Claire didn't have all the answers yet. But she wasn't disappearing anymore. She was starting to show up, not as who she was told to be but as who she really was.

That, too, was part of coming home to herself.

Grief: Mourning the Life You Didn't Choose

Grief isn't just about death. It's about the loss of what could have been. The life you imagined. The version of yourself you were taught to become. It's about mourning the future you were promised, the salvation, the eternal family, and the certainty that if you were faithful enough, everything would turn out right.

It's about grieving the roles you lived for, the dreams you carried, the security you built your life around, and realizing they were never truly yours to begin with. It's about grieving the person you might have become if you had been allowed to choose freely. The self that wasn't shaped by fear, obedience, and the need to earn love. The self that could have grown without conditions.

When you start to unravel your story and truly understand how deeply it shaped you, there's often a wave of grief that hits. It's disorienting to realize that the foundation you built your life on wasn't yours. And underneath that awareness, there's a deep, aching sorrow for the time you lost, the parts of yourself you abandoned, and the future you never got to live.

Sometimes, this grief rises later, after you have started to heal. You see it when you watch your children grow without the weight you carried. When you love them unconditionally. When you let them feel their anger, sadness, and joy without shame. When you celebrate their bodies, identities, and relationships without judgment. You see the freedom you are trying to give them, and you realize how little of it you were given. You realize what it means to belong without conditions. You realize what it means to be loved without needing to earn it.

And you grieve, not just for the life you were promised but for the life you might have had. For the self you might have been if you had been allowed to be fully human from the beginning.

This kind of grief is complex. It's layered. It doesn't follow a straight line. Some days you'll feel relief, even freedom. Other days, the weight of what's been lost might feel unbearable. Both are valid. Both are part of the process. Grieving the life you didn't choose doesn't mean you're ungrateful. It doesn't mean you regret everything that happened. It means you are finally telling the truth about what it costs to survive.

And if you were raised inside the LDS Church, grief can get even more complicated.

You were taught that righteousness would protect you. That if you made the right choices, followed the commandments, and stayed faithful enough, your life would turn out the way it was supposed to. That families could be eternal. That losses would only be temporary. That God had a plan, and if you trusted Him, everything would make sense in the end.

When pain came, you were given the language of certainty.

> *"Have an eternal perspective."*
> *"Trust in God's plan."*
> *"Be grateful you know the truth."*

Grief was supposed to be temporary. Manageable. An expression of faith, not despair. If you grieved too long or too hard, it was seen as weakness. A sign that your testimony wasn't strong enough.

You learned to package your grief into something palatable. To bear it with a smile. To call it a trial and move on.

But real grief doesn't work that way. Grief is not linear. It is not tidy. It does not submit to timelines or testimonies. It asks to be felt. To be honored. To be witnessed.

And when grief is denied, when it is covered over with certainty or spiritual slogans, it doesn't disappear. It goes underground. It turns into shame. Into loneliness. Into a quiet ache that says, "Something must be wrong with me."

Real grief work isn't about finding the silver lining. It's about making space for the full spectrum: sorrow, rage, confusion, numbness, and even moments of peace. It's about learning to trust that your grief is valid, even when it doesn't look like anyone else's. Even when it doesn't make sense. Even when no one else sees what you have lost.

***

Try This:

Sitting With One Piece of Grief

You do not have to name it all at once. You do not have to carry everything you lost at the same time. Start smaller. Start closer.

Think of one piece of grief.
Not the whole story.
Just one part.

Maybe it is the life you thought you were building.
Maybe it is the child you were before you learned to be small.
Maybe it is the future you thought obedience would give you.
Maybe it is the self you never got to know.

Choose one.
Hold it quietly for a moment.
Notice what it feels like.

You do not have to explain it.
You do not have to justify it.
You do not have to understand it.

Just stay with it.
Let yourself grieve this one small piece.

If it helps, write down a few words.
You could write a full letter about it—or not.
If you want to write, write about what was lost and for the part of you that remembers.

Grief is not something you finish.
It is something you learn how to hold, one breath, one memory, and one truth at a time.

***

Tip From a Therapist: The Grief You Didn't Expect

Sometimes, the most painful part of this process isn't the big moments. It's the quiet realizations. The sudden awareness that your life was built around someone else's rules. That the dreams you chased weren't really yours. That the love you received was conditional.

This kind of grief is often invisible to others. It's not about a clear loss they can see. It's about waking up to how much of yourself had to be hidden to stay safe, to be loved, to belong.

Let yourself grieve that. Grieve what you missed out on. Grieve the people who never really saw you. Grieve the moments you thought you were the problem when you were just trying to survive.

This grief is sacred. It clears space. It tells the truth. And it makes room for something new, not because you've forgotten what was lost but because you've made the brave choice to feel it.

***

She said no, and nothing bad happened. Her chest still tightened, and the guilt still came. But underneath it all, there was a small, steady exhale. A flicker of relief. Her body knew that it was okay to protect her own capacity.

Setting boundaries didn't come easily for Claire. She had spent so many years saying yes automatically that the idea of saying no felt like betrayal. Not just betrayal of others but betrayal of who she was supposed to be. The good daughter. The selfless wife. The reliable friend. The one who never needed too much. The one who never caused trouble.

The first time she said no, it was small. A neighbor asked her to organize a church activity, something she would have normally agreed to without thinking, even if she was already overwhelmed. But this time, she paused. She felt the exhaustion in her body. She felt the resentment rising before the word yes could slip out. And even though her heart pounded in her chest, she said, "I'm so sorry, but I can't take that on right now."

Her whole body rebelled the moment the words left her mouth. Her chest tightened. Her stomach twisted. The guilt came rushing in fast and hot, telling her she had disappointed someone, failed at being good.

Later, sitting in my office, she whispered, "It felt like I had done something wrong. Like I had let everyone down."

But she hadn't let anyone down. She had honored herself. And even though the guilt was loud, and the old beliefs were still pulling at her, there was a small, quiet part inside her that felt different. Stronger. More real.

That's how it begins. One small no at a time. Not perfectly. Not without fear. But with the slow, growing truth that your needs are not a betrayal.

***

Try This:

Think of a moment this week when you said yes but your body meant no.

What did you notice in your breath, your chest, your jaw?

What might it be like to pause next time and listen to that signal?

***

Boundaries and Reclaiming Autonomy

When you've spent your life constructing a reality based on someone else's expectations, it can be disorienting to realize the foundation wasn't truly yours. Every decision and every path you took was shaped by what was considered acceptable, righteous, or safe. And now, as you begin to untangle from that, you're faced with a different task: building something new, this time on your own terms.

But here's the thing. When you've been taught that your worth is tied to how much you give, how well you serve, or how little space you take up, asserting your needs can feel foreign. Even wrong. Saying no might trigger guilt. Resting might feel selfish. Setting a boundary might feel like betrayal. Not because it is but because those were the messages you internalized.

This is why reclaiming agency is so important and so hard. It's not just about learning how to choose. It's about learning that you're allowed to. That your needs matter. That your no is valid. That your voice belongs to you.

As you grow, people around you will notice. Some may celebrate it. Some may resist it. And some relationships may shift or even end. That doesn't mean you're doing it wrong. It means the system is adjusting to your truth. And truth will always disrupt what was built on silence.

You might feel the discomfort of others. You might feel their disappointment or confusion. But their discomfort isn't your responsibility. Your job isn't to keep everyone else comfortable. Your job is to honor your own reality.

Boundaries aren't about shutting people out. They're about protecting what's sacred. They're about choosing what's okay with you and what's not. Even if that's brand new territory. Especially if it is.

***

Try This: Noticing the Body's Boundary Signals

You don't have to wait for the perfect moment to start setting boundaries. You can begin by noticing the signals your body is already giving you.

The next time you feel a yes or no rising in your body, pause.

Ask yourself:

- What happens in my body when I want to say no but feel pressure to say yes?

- Does my chest tighten? Does my jaw clench? Do I hold my breath?

- What stories or fears come up at that moment?

Let yourself stay with the feeling for just a few seconds longer than usual. Then ask:

- What do I actually want right now?

- What would it feel like to honor that?

If you decide to say no, notice what shifts:

- Does your body soften?

- Is there guilt? Relief? A deeper breath?

You don't have to get it right every time. Just keep listening. Boundaries begin in the body, long before the words are spoken.

Try This - Setting Boundaries: The External Expression of Agency

With internal agency comes external action. Boundaries are how we express our truth out loud. They're the no when you mean no. The pause when you need space. The decision to rest when you're tired. The choice to stop performing and start honoring your own needs.

If this is new, it might feel uncomfortable at first. That's okay. Here are a few ways to practice:

Start Small
Begin with low-stakes situations to get used to using your voice. Decline a social invitation. Ask for a different seat. State a preference, even if it feels small.

Anticipate Reactions
Some people might not respond well, especially if they were benefiting from your lack of boundaries. That doesn't mean you did something wrong. It means the dynamics are shifting.

Seek Support
Surround yourself with people who respect your boundaries and remind you that you're allowed to have them. These people can help ground you when guilt creeps in.

Reflect and Adjust
After you set a boundary, notice how it felt. What worked? What didn't? What did your body say afterward?

Did your body feel more grounded or more tense afterward? These cues help you learn what safe connection feels like.

Use that information to keep learning what safety and alignment feel like in real time.

Boundaries are a skill and a practice. You don't have to get them perfect. You just have to keep listening for what's true.

***

Therapist Tip: Boundaries Will Ruffle Feathers, and That's Okay

One of the hardest parts of this work is that healing changes your relationships. When you stop abandoning yourself, it changes how people experience you. Some might pull closer. Others might get defensive, confused, or upset. That's not a reflection of your worth. It's a reflection of the system recalibrating.

Setting boundaries might feel like you're doing something wrong. But often, that's just your nervous system reacting to something unfamiliar. If you were raised to believe that love meant self-sacrifice, then saying no might feel like a rupture. If you were praised for being low-maintenance, then expressing a need might feel like a risk.

But here's the truth. Your discomfort isn't a red flag. It's a sign that you're doing something different. You're interrupting old patterns. You're honoring the parts of you that never got protected before.

It's okay if other people are uncomfortable. It's okay if they don't understand. That's not yours to carry. What matters most is that you're learning to stay with yourself and choose what's real and right for you.

***

Sometimes, the rupture doesn't come with anger or even sadness. It comes with numbness. Disconnection. The quiet grief of not knowing how to want or how to feel safe in your skin. That's where Hannah began.

Her name was Hannah. She had grown up believing that if she did everything right, marriage would be easy. That she would be ready for marriage. That sex would feel sacred, spiritual, and pure. That love would erase any fear she carried.

She stayed faithful. She saved herself. She followed every rule she had been given.

But when the moment came, her body didn't feel sacred. It felt frozen. Tight. Afraid.

She thought something was wrong with her. Maybe she was broken. Maybe she wasn't worthy of the love she had been promised. No one had told her that years of fear could not be undone with a ceremony. No one had prepared her for what it would feel like to be a stranger inside her own skin.

In therapy, Hannah struggled to explain what was happening. She didn't feel angry at first. She didn't even feel sad. She just felt numb. Like her body wasn't really hers. Like she had been following the path she was supposed to, but somewhere along the way, she had lost herself.

Healing didn't start with fixing sex. It didn't even start with wanting more. It started smaller. Softer. It started with standing in the sunlight and letting herself notice what it felt like to be warm. It started with touching her own hand and feeling the texture of her skin without judgment. It started with lying still and letting her body exist without expectation, without performance.

Hannah wasn't learning how to want more. She was learning that her body wasn't the enemy. That desire wasn't dangerous. That she didn't have to earn the right to feel safe inside her body.

It was slow. It was uncomfortable. It didn't feel sacred or beautiful at first. But it was real. It was hers. And piece by piece, Hannah was learning that coming home to her body wasn't a betrayal. It was healing.

Hannah's story isn't rare. It's one of the most common things I see in women who were taught to equate worth with purity. She did everything right. She followed the rules. And still, when the moment came, her body said no. Not because she was broken but because no one ever told her that fear can live in the body long after the fear-based teachings are gone.

That's the thing about religious trauma. It doesn't always look like a crisis. Sometimes it looks like going through the motions, feeling numb, feeling disconnected, not knowing how to want or ask or feel. It looks like standing in your own life and wondering why something feels missing.

If this is your story or even part of it, you're not alone. Reclaiming your relationship with your body and your pleasure isn't about doing it right. It's about healing the rupture that taught you your body was dangerous. It's about learning that you don't have to disappear to be safe.

Reclaiming Sexuality and Pleasure

It's hard to talk about pleasure when your body has always felt like it belonged to someone else. When you were taught that desire is dangerous. That your worth depends on purity, on virtue. That your value to a future partner or to God was directly tied to what you did or didn't do with your body.

This part of the work can be tender. You may feel grief. Shame. Disconnection. You may not even know what you want because you were never allowed to ask. And when you did feel desire, curiosity, or pleasure, it probably came with guilt. Or fear. Or the need to hide it.

Purity culture doesn't just teach abstinence. It teaches self-erasure. It tells you that your body is a threat. That you are responsible for someone else's thoughts. That your sexuality is something to control, protect, or give away. Never something that belongs to you.

So even the idea of reconnecting with pleasure can feel overwhelming. It might not feel like something you're allowed to have. It might feel like crossing a line. Like it's unsafe. That's why reclaiming pleasure can be such a radical part of healing. It's not just about sex. It's about learning to trust yourself again. To trust your body. Your boundaries. Your wanting.

Pleasure work matters not because you need to be sexual but because you deserve to feel safe and at home in your body. You get to reclaim your relationship with desire, whether that comes through touch, connection, sensuality, intimacy, or simply presence. You get to be curious. To notice what feels good. What feels off. What feels like yours.

Reclaiming sexuality isn't about becoming someone different. It's about returning to yourself. To the version of you who was always there underneath the shame. The one who gets to feel joy. Connection. And yes, even pleasure, without fear.

You're allowed to want. You're allowed to feel. You're allowed to explore. Not because you're broken or need fixing but because you're healing. Because you're finally safe enough to ask what you want instead of only doing what you were told you should want.

***

Try This: Reclaiming Pleasure, Bit by Bit

You don't have to be ready to explore sexuality to begin this work. Start smaller. Start slower. Start where you are.

Begin with sensation
Pick one simple moment in your day. Drinking tea. Stepping into the sun. Running your hands under warm water. Pause. Let yourself notice what it feels like. Do you tense? Do you soften? Can you stay with it, even for just one breath longer than usual?

Ask yourself: What feels good?
Not what you've been told is okay. Not what you're supposed to want. Just what feels good in your body, in your skin, in this moment. That might be a soft blanket, a long walk, or a song that moves you. Let it be yours.

Notice the voice that tries to shut it down
It might say it's selfish. Or wrong. Or too much. You don't have to silence that voice. Just notice it. Ask yourself, Whose voice is that? What was I taught this means about me? Then gently offer yourself something kinder.

Let pleasure be safe again
Try placing one hand on your chest or belly and simply being with yourself. Feel the rise and fall. Notice how it feels to slow down. This, too, is a kind of pleasure, being present in your body on your terms.

Remember, this isn't about pushing past shame or fixing anything. It's about making space. About allowing curiosity. About practicing what it means to feel at home in yourself.

***

Tip From a Therapist: Go at Your Pace

If exploring pleasure brings up fear, guilt, or overwhelm, that's not a sign you're doing it wrong. It's a sign your system is protecting you. Go slow. Let safety lead. You don't need to push past the discomfort. You just need to stay connected while gently expanding what feels safe and possible.

Your body might not know that it's safe yet. That's okay. This work isn't about forcing your way forward. It's about honoring where you are and building trust with your body one moment at a time.

When Your Body Says No

Remember that trauma lives not just in memory but in the body. For many women and nonbinary people, one of the most common and least talked about expressions of this is **vaginismus**, the involuntary tightening of the vaginal muscles that can make penetration painful or impossible.

This is not a failure. It is not your fault. It is a trauma response. It is your body's way of protecting you when no one else does. Often, it's rooted in fear, shame, purity teachings, or years of disconnection from your desire.

Healing vaginismus isn't about pushing through. It's about slowing down. Working with a trauma-informed specialist who understands both the emotional and physiological layers of this experience is an important part of healing. With time, safety, and support, your body can learn what's safe again.

And you get to be the one who decides.

***

For Claire, the changes started small. She noticed which friendships felt harder now.The ones where she had always been the one listening, accommodating, and smoothing everything over. When she started showing up differently, she was a little more honest and less willing to disappear. Some people leaned in closer. Others pulled away.

At first, the distance felt like failure. Like she had broken something by needing too much. But slowly, she realized it was something else. She wasn't breaking anything. She was seeing clearly for the first time.

Some connections could stretch and hold the real her.

Some could not.

And even when it was the right choice, sometimes it still hurt.

Sometimes, it was still a loss.

But it was also part of finding her way back to herself.

Connection and Relationships

Healing doesn't mean doing it all alone. But part of healing is learning how to show up for yourself fully, honestly, and without apology. And when you do, things start to change. Because when you stop hiding the parts of you that were silenced, the relationships around you start to shift too.

Sometimes that shift is painful. You begin to see the patterns you used to miss. You realize you were the one holding everything together by staying small. That you were chosen for how well you followed the rules, not for who you really were. As you grow, not everyone will grow with you. Some relationships stretch. Some fade. Some end.

That doesn't mean you're doing it wrong. It means you're finally showing up as yourself.

When you've lived through religious trauma, connection becomes complicated. Many of us were taught that love means sacrifice. That our job is to serve, give, and make others okay, even if it costs us everything. We were praised for being agreeable, quiet, selfless, and obedient. That wasn't love. That was role fulfillment. And it often meant outsourcing our worth to someone else.

So when you start reclaiming your voice, needs, and body, your relationships will feel different too. And they should. Because once you stop abandoning yourself, you also stop tolerating the kind of connection that requires your silence.

Healthy connection isn't about shrinking to fit. It's not about losing yourself to belong. It's about being with people who make space for your whole self, your needs, your no, your growth, and your joy. It won't always be easy. But it will be mutual. It will be safe. It will feel like home, not like a performance.

You get to ask:

- Do I feel more myself in this relationship or less?

- Can I be honest here? Can I say no here? Can I be soft here?

- Do I feel safe enough to grow here?

Healing changes how we relate. Not overnight. But steadily. You stop chasing what harms you. You begin to notice who feels safe in your nervous system, not just in your thoughts. You learn to build relationships rooted in truth, reciprocity, and care. Not fear. Not duty. Not performance.

As Hannah reconnected with her body, she also began to name what she needed. At first, that felt risky, like she was breaking the rules of who she was supposed to be. And not everyone understood. Some relationships couldn't hold the changes she was making. Some faded. Some quietly fell away. But when she let herself be seen in her marriage, something different happened. Her husband didn't pull away. He leaned in. Slowly, he began learning how to hold space for her needs, her truth, and the real version of her that was emerging. Their relationship changed, not because it was easy but because it was honest. And in that honesty, intimacy started to grow. Not from performance but from presence.

***

Try This: Noticing the Shape of Your Relationships

As you show up more fully, your relationships will shift. Some will deepen. Some will stretch. Some may fall away. That doesn't mean you're failing. It means you're healing.

Take time to reflect:

- Where do I feel the most like myself?

- Who gives me space to say no, change, and grow?

- Where do I shrink to keep the peace or perform to be accepted?

Try one small shift. Say something true, even if it's quiet. Let yourself take up a little more space. Choose rest instead of obligation. Then notice what happens.

Let it be information. You don't have to decide anything yet. You're just gathering data. What does this relationship feel like in your body?

What do you notice after being with this person? Do you feel more grounded or more scattered? More seen or more invisible?

If something feels tender or hard, name that too. This part often brings grief. You might mourn the version of a relationship you hoped for. Or the one you pretended you had. That grief is real. It deserves to be honored.

***

Tip from a Therapist: Grief Is Part of the Process

This might be one of the most painful parts of healing, showing up more fully in your relationships, and realizing they were never built to hold the real you. You didn't know it at the time. You were surviving. You were doing what you were taught.

But now, as you come home to yourself, the cracks start to show. The connection you thought was solid suddenly feels hollow. The love you relied on begins to feel like performance, not presence.

Let yourself grieve that. Grieve the years you spent contorting yourself to be accepted. Grieve the people who loved the version of you that was never fully true. Grieve what never was.

This grief isn't a detour. It's part of the work. It clears space for something deeper. Something real. Something reciprocal. Healing teaches you how to stay connected to yourself and, from that place, build relationships that can support you.

***

Not a Straight Line

This work isn't linear. It's layered. You don't move cleanly from beliefs to emotions to the body to identity and arrive at some final place. You loop back. You revisit old places with new eyes. You notice things you couldn't see before. And every time you do, you meet yourself with a little more honesty, a little more compassion.

Healing isn't about becoming someone else. It's about reclaiming the parts of you that had to go quiet to stay safe. The parts that were silenced to belong. The parts that are still here, waiting for you to come back.

There's no one right way to do this. There's no perfect timeline. There's no map that fits everyone.

Some of this work you'll do quietly on your own, in your journal, in your thoughts, in the sacred privacy of your body beginning to feel again. Some of it will happen in community, with trusted friends, shared stories, or spaces where others nod before you even finish the sentence. And some of it may ask for deeper support. For the presence of a therapist, a guide, someone trained to help you hold the weight that feels too heavy to carry alone. Needing help does not mean you have failed. It means you are human.

But there are tools. There are practices. There are gentle ways to begin listening again, to your body, your voice, your grief, and your longing again. There are ways to rebuild from the inside out, slowly and intentionally, in a way that finally fits the real you.

You get to decide what you need. You get to choose when you're ready. You get to ask your own questions. You get to build a life that doesn't require you to disappear to belong. And you are already further than you think.

Becoming whole isn't something you finish. It's something you lean into, over and over again.

You do not have to have it all figured out today. You are already doing the work every time you listen, every time you stay with yourself a little longer.

Chapter 9

Holding Religious Trauma in the Therapy Room

I f you're here, reading this chapter, it's likely because you've been sitting with clients who are carrying deep religious pain or maybe because you've felt it yourself. You're here because you want to do this well. Because you know it matters how you show up in these moments. And you're right; it does.

This chapter isn't a checklist. It's an invitation. To pause. To get honest. To learn. To ask yourself not just what you know but how you show up. Because this work, this kind of pain, asks more of us.

Religious trauma isn't just about belief. It's about identity, safety, family, love, worthiness, the body, and the soul. It's layered. And it rarely exists in isolation. Religious trauma often overlaps with other identities and systems including gender, sexuality, race, neurodivergence, disability, and class. These intersections shape how harm is experienced and how healing unfolds. You can't just look at the spiritual narrative. You have to consider the full, layered story your client is carrying. And when someone starts to open that up in your office, how you respond matters. It matters more than you think.

It's also easy to underestimate the weight of your reactions in the room. Your body, your story, your beliefs, all of it shows up. That's countertransference. That's bias. It's not something to fear, but it is something to notice. And for many therapists, religious belief systems aren't viewed as something that can shape countertransference or even as something that should be examined. But they live in us, often deeply. If you're unaware of how your internal responses are being activated, you might respond from your discomfort instead of their story.

This isn't about having the right answers. It's about being able to stay present when things get complicated. To listen. To not look away. To hold space for your clients no matter what they choose or don't choose. That's what this work takes.

Understanding the Spectrum of Religious Belief

To do this work well, we need language for the different ways people relate to religion. Not just what they believe but how close they are to the system. How deeply it shaped them. How far they've moved from it or how much they still feel tethered to it, even if they no longer believe.

This isn't a linear journey. People shift across time. They may cling tighter when harm happens or walk away quietly when no one notices they're missing. They may live in two places at once, holding onto pieces of faith that still feel beautiful while also grieving what's been lost. Understanding that range helps you meet your client where they actually are, not where you assume they are.

What follows is a map. Not to box people in but to give language to experiences that often go unnamed. These positions aren't steps, and they're not goals. They're simply ways of relating to faith, identity, and belonging. And knowing where your client is on this map, along with where you are, can change the work completely.

These five positions describe common ways people relate to faith and religious belief systems. They are not linear. You might move through them in different orders, revisit the same place more than once, or live in more than one at the same time. You might also only ever identify with one. And that's valid too.

Where someone lands can shift based on their phase of life, their relationships, their access to safety, or the presence of harm and healing. What they needed in one season may not be what they need in another.

There is no right way to do this. There is only their way.

The Spectrum of Religious Belief

A clinical map for holding religious identity in the therapy room

1. Devout / Deeply Religious / Orthodox

The system feels whole. Beliefs are internalized as absolute truth. There's often a deep sense of identity, belonging, and purpose. Questions may arise, but they are typically met with faith, obedience, or increased devotion.

Key themes: Certainty; alignment; belonging; obedience; suppressed doubt; perfectionism; gendered/social expectations; religion becomes identity

Example language:
"I know this church is true."
"I just need to have more faith."
"If I follow the commandments, everything will work out."

2. Ex-Religious / Post-Religious / Non-Religious

This is a settled departure or someone who isn't closely tied to religion anymore. Some feel peace. Some still carry pain. Some aren't connected at all to religion. Many reclaim autonomy, rebuild values, or let go of religion entirely. Previous religions frameworks no longer define their current framework.

Key themes: Personal autonomy and agency; personal morality; finding peace, neutrality, or disconnection from religion; letting go of the need for certainty; building or embracing new spiritual/secular frameworks

Example language:

"I'm not religious anymore."

"I'm finding my own way now."

"It still hurts, but I know I can't go back."

3. Progressive / Reforming / Deconstructing

Part of a religious group, but challenges some of the beliefs or cultural norms. Sometimes has growing tension or unresolved problems. Many feel committed to changing the system from within or struggle to find an identity outside of the system. Can be a transitory phase, as some reconsider their beliefs within the system or leave it and rebuild their identity outside of it.

Key themes: Nuance; advocacy; integrity; spiritual conflict; lack of belonging; worth; safety; community; authenticity; internal conflict; trust-seeking; grief.

Example language:

"I still believe, but I don't agree with everything."

"I want to change it from the inside."

"It's not all bad."

"There is still good in the church."

"Everything I believed is falling apart."
"I feel like I don't even know who I am anymore."

4. Cultural / Passive

Religion is more of a cultural identity than a core identity. Individuals may attend for family or tradition. Personal convictions may change over time. There may be connections to rituals, language, or community. Some avoid rather than confront internal and cultural religious conflicts.

Key themes: Heritage, continuity, ambiguity, job/family/social expectation

Example language:
"I don't really believe it, but I still go with my family."
"It's just part of who I am."
"I'm not religious, but I still say I am."
"It's my community."

Understanding your own relationship with religion helps you meet your clients with more precision and care. It also helps you check your own reactions because you likely have a spot on this spectrum too. And that will shape how you respond, whether you mean to or not.

You may not always hear these distinctions named out loud, especially in communities where one belief system is dominant. In some traditions, there's often a binary mindset: you're either all in or all out. If you're not a true believer, you're lumped in with everyone who has left, is questioning, or doesn't fit the mold. This can make it harder for clients or for therapists to name where they actually are or even know that a spectrum exists. But it's there. And if you're doing trauma work, being able to recognize your religious bias and work within this spectrum of belief matters deeply.

Knowing where you fall on this spectrum and how your beliefs have shaped the way you respond matters as you move through the rest of this chapter. Some parts may challenge you more than others. If you feel reactive or defensive, that doesn't mean you're doing it wrong. That's the place to pause. That's your invitation. That's where your work begins.

And remember, there is no single path. You might stay in one place. You might move slowly or shift again and again. None of that means you're behind. None of that means you're broken. There is space for clarity, healing, and wholeness wherever you land, as long as it feels true to you.

Trauma-Informed Care

Religious trauma isn't something you push someone through. It's something you sit with. Witness. Walk beside. It's slow. It's layered. It asks for attunement and responsiveness, not urgency or assumption.

This kind of work can't be about your goals. It can't be about what you think healing should look like or how quickly you think they should get there. Trauma-informed care means they get to decide what feels safe, what's worth exploring, and what they're not ready to touch yet.

Start with where they are. Not where you want them to be.

That might mean working with someone who still believes deeply. Or someone who isn't sure what they believe anymore. Or someone who never had language for what they went through until now. It all counts. It all matters.

And here's the part that's hard for a lot of therapists, especially if you've done your own deconstructing: You don't get to decide what your client's relationship with their faith should look like. Not now. Not later. Not ever.

A client might process deep trauma from inside their faith and still choose to stay. Another might walk away completely. Another might land somewhere in between. That doesn't make one outcome more successful or more healed than another. It just makes it *theirs*.

Trauma-informed care is about pacing. Consent. Respect. It's about knowing that the goal isn't "recovery from religion." The goal is their autonomy. Their clarity. Their emotional safety. You don't lead them out. You support them in making meaning, setting boundaries, and reconnecting to their own sense of self, on their terms.

Sometimes, that means you go slow. Sometimes, it means you pause. And sometimes, it means you sit in silence with a story that still has no words.

And when we don't know what to say or when the silence feels too big, we often reach for something that sounds helpful. That's where spiritual bypassing can sneak in.

Spiritual Bypassing

Spiritual bypassing is when we use spiritual language, beliefs, or practices to avoid emotional pain, dismiss struggle, or minimize trauma. It can sound hopeful. It can even come with the best of intentions. But when used in the therapy room, it often skips over the real story. It shuts the door on complexity and moves away from the wound instead of toward it.

Here's the thing, bypassing isn't always obvious. Sometimes, it's loud and overt. Sometimes, it's subtle. A quiet shift. A change in tone. A pause that skips too quickly into positivity. Here are a few ways it can show up:

- "God gives the hardest battles to His strongest soldiers."

- "Everything happens for a reason."

- "You're stronger because of what you went through."

- "That's not the gospel. The gospel is love."

- "But look at the good it brought you."

- "Maybe this was part of God's plan to help you grow."

Sometimes, the client says it. Sometimes, you say it. Either way, it's important to ask what purpose it's serving at that moment. Is it creating space for deeper exploration, or is it closing the door on pain?

In trauma-informed work, we don't rush regulation. We don't rush meaning. We don't reframe before we validate. And we don't prioritize hope at the cost of honesty. Spiritual bypassing often does all of those things. It pulls us toward comfort instead of truth.

If you find yourself wanting to make it better, to soften it, to pivot to something redemptive, pause. That moment might be a chance to stay with what's real. Not to fix it. Not to spiritualize it. Just to witness it. That's the work.

Adaptive Belief or Bypassing?

Not every spiritual or hopeful statement is bypassing. Sometimes it's exactly what a client needs to say, believe, or hold onto. The key difference is whether it's being used to avoid the pain or whether it's grown from within it.

There's a point in trauma work when a client starts to make meaning. To integrate. To say things like:

- "What I went through was really hard. And I'm stronger because of it."

- "It broke something in me, but I also found something I didn't know I had."

- "I wouldn't choose it, but I can see how it shaped me."

These aren't always bypasses. They can be signs of healing. Of post-traumatic learning. Of adaptive belief. But only if they're coming from the client's own sense of timing and truth, not from pressure, discomfort, or someone else needing to tie it up with a bow.

A trauma-informed approach doesn't shut these statements down. But it does listen closely. It asks: *Does this belief feel empowering, or is it protecting them from something that's still too painful to touch?*

Sometimes, a client isn't ready to be in full grief or rage. Sometimes, this kind of meaning makes the pain tolerable for now. That's not a problem. That's pacing. That's survival. That's part of the process.

Your role is to witness, not to steer. To hold the space open, even when it's uncertain.

Start Where They Are

It sounds simple. But it's not.

Start where they are. Not where you think they should be. Not where your story wants to take them. Where *they* are.

That might be deep inside their faith. It might be halfway out. It might be in a place of numbness, anger, shame, or total collapse. It might not even have words yet. Maybe it's just a quiet moment, a question they're scared to say out loud. That's where you start.

Starting where they are means letting go of timelines. Letting go of your own urgency. It means remembering that just because someone isn't naming it the way you would doesn't mean they aren't holding it. It also means knowing that trauma healing isn't linear. Sometimes, they'll move forward and then pull back. Sometimes, it'll feel like nothing's happening. But their nervous system is tracking safety. And that matters more than insight.

You don't get to drag someone through this work. You don't get to rush it. What you *do* get to do is sit with them in it. Make space. Let them find their own language. If they say "the Spirit," say "the Spirit." If they say "God betrayed me," don't soften it. Don't make it easier. Stay there. Let it be what it is.

Start with the story as they know it. Not the version you think it's going to become. That's how you build trust. That's how you stay grounded in their process, not yours.

Spirituality as a Resource

When I think about spirituality now, I don't think about church pews or reverent prayers. I think about standing in the desert, sun on my face, surrounded by red rocks that feel older than language. I think about stillness. About the kind of quiet that settles inside your bones. About those moments where the world feels bigger than me, but I don't feel small. I fully belong.

That's spirituality to me. Not a set of beliefs but a sense of connection. Of belonging to something deeper.

And for a lot of clients, that kind of connection is still there, somewhere. Even after the trauma. Even when the religion that taught them to pray also taught them they were never enough.

Spirituality can still be a resource. But only if it comes from them. Not from you. Not from the system that hurt them. Not from the pressure to reclaim something before they're ready.

For some, it's still God. For others, it's breathwork or trees or music or moonlight or grief rituals passed down through generations. Sometimes it's something they're just beginning to imagine for themselves. And sometimes, it's silence.

Your job isn't to lead them toward or away from anything. Your job is to create enough safety for whatever shows up to have space.

If they want to revisit old prayers and see if they still fit, be there. If they want to scream at the sky and say they were lied to, be there for that too. If they don't want to talk about it at all, just breathe beside them.

There's no right spiritual path after religious trauma. There's just what feels true. What feels safe. What brings someone back to themselves.

And if spirituality starts to rise again in the healing, however it looks, honor it. Let it unfold on their terms. Not because it's the goal but because it belongs to them now.

It Was Never Just Religion

Most clients come in thinking they're wrestling with faith. But as the work unfolds, it becomes clear they're also wrestling with patriarchy. With whiteness. With capitalism. With the systems that shaped what their religion taught them was good, worthy, and true. It was never just about belief. It was about power.

You start to notice how patriarchy lives in the language of submission and modesty. How whiteness shows up in what was labeled "pure" or "worthy." How capitalism got woven into ideas of hard work, divine reward, and earned value. You start to realize that what was called sacred might also be tangled in supremacy.

And suddenly, it's not just your faith that's unraveling. It's the whole framework that held it up.

Clients might say, *"If this wasn't true, what else isn't?"* or *"I used to believe I had to be silent to be good, and now I can't stop seeing that message everywhere."*

That's not a failure of faith. That's a deeper kind of seeing.

This is often where the grief deepens. Where the anger comes in. Where your client starts to name not just spiritual harm but systemic harm, layers of gender, race, class, neurodivergence, and body-based shame that were all wrapped in religious authority.

And this is also where some therapists start to pull back. Because naming systems can feel like too much. Too political. Too big. Too far from the individual story.

But here's the thing, this *is* their individual story. It's all part of the same wound.

You don't have to be an expert in every system. But you do have to be willing to look. To check your own positioning. To notice where you hold privilege. Where you've benefited from the same systems your client is now trying to unlearn. That discomfort? That's part of the work too.

And not everyone will go there. Some stay focused on the spiritual harm. That's still real. Still sacred work. The point isn't to get them somewhere else; it's to stay with whatever is true for them.

Religious trauma isn't just about belief. It's about the frameworks that shaped how someone saw themselves and how they were seen.

When a client starts to see that, they're not just unlearning a religion. They're rebuilding an entire sense of self. One that deserves to be seen clearly, held gently, and never rushed.

Are You Still Aligned With the Faith?

If you're someone who still finds alignment with your religion or faith, this next part might ask more of you. Because when a client starts to name harm within a belief system you still hold dearly, it's not just about what they're saying. It's about how it lands in your body.

You might notice that religious part of you rise up first. That makes sense. But what you do with it matters.

Can you take a breath and step back? Can you stay grounded and present with your client's story, even if it's different or even opposite from your own?

Ask yourself honestly:

- Do I ever find myself defending the religion or the culture?

- Do I say things like, "That's not the religion. That's just the culture"? Or, "That's not what they actually believe." Or even, "I'm sorry you had that experience. Religion can be so powerful and healing," or "The gospel is perfect, even if the people aren't"?

These kinds of statements might feel true. They might even be comforting to you. And it's true. There is research showing that for many people, religion and spirituality can be protective factors, sources of strength, and important parts of healing. But that does not take away from the reality that for others, those same systems caused harm. The impact is not just in the teaching itself. It's in how it was delivered, how it was internalized, and whether it made space for the person to be fully human.

So when you say something like, "Religion can be so powerful and healing," the real question becomes: are you saying it to make room for your client's truth? Or are you saying it to ease your own discomfort? In the context of religious trauma, even well-intentioned comments can close a door instead of opening one. They can mirror the same spiritual bypassing that your client is trying to name and unravel.

And it's important to remember not every client receives the same message in the same way. A teaching about modesty, obedience, or worthiness can land differently for a queer teen, a neurodivergent child, or a woman of color. The harm gets filtered through identity, through visibility, and through power. What felt beautiful or neutral to you may have carried shame, silencing, or fear for someone else. And sometimes, even between two people who appear to share all the same privileges, the impact still differs. Because trauma is not just about what was said or done. It's about what it meant, how it landed, and what it cost.

The work is to stay with your client. To keep their story centered over your own. To notice when your discomfort or defensiveness shows up and to explore that, not act from it. This is a form of counter-transference, something to watch for when your client's story bumps up against your belief system. Awareness of your reactions isn't just helpful; it's necessary to do this work ethically and responsibly.

There's a bigger question worth sitting with: Can you ethically support someone who is deconstructing a system you're still actively in? Maybe yes. Maybe no. But if you feel yourself challenging this question or getting defensive reading this, that probably tells you something. That subtle shift into defense or redirection might signal a personal belief, a bias, or even a form of countertransference. It could also be an emotional reaction tied to your own story. Whatever it is, it's worth exploring with curiosity. If left unchecked, it can shape the way you respond, what you validate, and how safe the space truly feels for your client.

And here's something else: If you're going to do this work well, you have to understand both perspectives. What it feels like from inside the religion and how it looks from the outside. The internal logic. The pressure. The longing. The fear. The meaning behind certain phrases or practices. Without that, you risk missing the depth of what your client is carrying.

Are You Deconstructing?

For many therapists drawn to this work, the pull is personal. You're not just hearing your clients' stories. You're seeing pieces of your own. And that can be powerful. It can also get blurry.

Deconstruction changes you. It changes how you see systems, relationships, identity, and even time. And when you're in the middle of it or still sorting through the pieces, it can be easy to overidentify with your clients. To think, *I know exactly what this is,* or *I've been there.*

Sometimes that resonance is helpful. It creates safety. It allows for deep understanding. But it can also lead to enmeshment, over-disclosure, or unconsciously moving someone through your healing map instead of theirs.

Ask yourself honestly:

- Am I reacting to my client's story, or am I remembering my own?

- Do I feel the urge to give advice, protect them, or push them forward?

- Can I let their process be different from mine, even if I think I know where it's going?

- Am I overidentifying with the emotion in the room? The

rage, the grief, or the fear? Can I hold it without being consumed by it?

You don't have to be done deconstructing to do this work. But you do have to stay aware. Triggers can still sneak up on you. A new talk at a conference, a change in church leadership, a life transition, or any moment can stir something unexpected. Old grief, fresh anger, things you thought were settled. Sometimes, that means you need to step back. Not forever, just long enough to ground yourself again. That's not a failure. That's part of doing this work responsibly.

And when that happens, you need support. You need to keep yourself in check.

This is where good consultation matters. Where supervision that includes your own spiritual story matters. Where you pause when you feel activated and ask, *Is this about them, or is this about me?*

The more clarity you have around your story, the more capacity you'll have to hold theirs without confusion or entanglement. This is where those lines can blur, transference, countertransference, and the emotional charge that comes with deep identification. Being able to step back and sort through it is what keeps the work safe for both of you.

When You Don't Share the Experience

You don't have to have lived it to hold it well. That's true in all trauma work, and it's true here too. But religious trauma can stir something different in the therapy room. Especially when it touches on beliefs, language, or systems you've never been part of or that you've never questioned.

If you've never been in a high-demand religion or never been taught to tie your worth to obedience, you might miss how deep this goes. It's easy to think, *Why didn't they just leave?* or *That sounds like a bad church experience, not trauma.* You might not say that out loud. But if that thought is sitting in the back of your mind, it's going to show up in the room.

It's important to educate yourself. Read. Listen. Ask questions. But don't assume that what you've learned from TikTok or Reddit or someone else's story applies directly to the person in front of you. Learn how *your client* experienced it. What shaped them. What stayed in their body. What hurt the most. That's the story that matters.

Here's what matters more than understanding: curiosity. The willingness to stay open. To not minimize what you don't understand. To reflect on your discomfort instead of pushing it away or covering it with silver linings.

Clients don't need you to know what it was like. They need you to believe them. To take their story seriously. To not rush in with solutions or theological reframes. To not make it about what you think you would have done.

This work doesn't require shared belief. It requires respect. And a commitment to keep learning.

Role of the Therapist

You're not here to fix it. You're not here to convert, correct, or lead someone out. You're here to sit with what's in front of you. The unraveling. The ache. The stories that still feel tender, sacred, or both. That's the job. And it sounds simple, but it's not.

Religious trauma doesn't just live in belief. It shows up in the nervous system. In regulation. In attachment. In the way someone sees themselves or can't trust their voice. When someone starts to talk about it, they're not just questioning faith; they're opening the door to everything that held it in place. And what you do with that story matters.

This work asks more from us. It asks for steadiness. For honesty. For the ability to sit with not knowing. You don't get to pull someone through their process. You don't get to decide where they land. You walk beside them. That's it. And that's everything.

You have to track your reactions. Know when something bumps into your story. Notice when your body wants to shut down or make it better. That's part of the work too. Noticing. Getting support. Naming what's yours and what isn't.

You don't have to be perfect. You just have to be real. Present. Grounded enough to hold space without filling it. And willing to treat what they're sharing like something sacred, even if it no longer fits in a sacred box.

Doing the Work Behind the Work

This work holds weight. Not just for your client but for you. And being a safe therapist for someone navigating religious trauma means more than being kind or curious. It means knowing yourself. It means knowing your limits. It means being honest about what you can and can't hold. It also means doing your own work outside of session and ongoing.

Clients coming out of systems rooted in power are already vulnerable. They've been taught to defer to authority. To silence their knowing. That pattern doesn't disappear when they enter your office. If anything, it can get stronger. And if you're not paying attention, you might unknowingly step into the role they were trying to leave behind.

This doesn't mean you can't have opinions. Or boundaries. It means you can't use your role to guide someone toward what *you* think is right, spiritually, emotionally, or relationally. You are not their new source of truth. You are a witness. A reflector. A steady, regulated presence.

That presence requires internal work. You need to be aware of your countertransference, biases, and emotional reactions. You need to be tracking when your urgency is taking over, your story is showing up, or you're offering clarity that wasn't asked for. You need support. Supervision. Spaces where you can keep sorting through your relationship with belief, systems, and power.

Being safe doesn't mean being perfect. It means being accountable. It means knowing when you've missed something and being willing to repair it. It means continuing to do your work so your client doesn't have to carry it for you.

You don't have to have it all figured out. But if you're going to do this work, you have to stay awake. You have to keep learning. You have to be willing to step back and check in with yourself again and again.

Not because you've figured it all out. But because you're willing to keep showing up with clarity, with honesty, and with care.

Holding Space

This work is not simple. It is layered, heavy, and full of complexity. People are carrying stories that were never meant to be carried alone. They are carrying systems of oppression, generations of wounds, and fear inside their bodies and their bones.

Your work is not to fix it. Your work is to sit with it. To witness the ache, to honor the grief, the anger, the confusion, without rushing to make it neat. Healing does not happen because you know all the right things. Healing happens in the presence of someone who stays.

It will not always be clear. You will not always have the perfect words. But if you can keep showing up with humility and care, if you can stay curious and grounded and human, you will make a difference. You will help create the conditions for safety, for trust, for healing to take root.

This work asks a lot of us. But it also offers something back. The quiet beauty of watching someone come home to themselves. The privilege of witnessing strength that was there all along. The reminder that healing is possible, even in places once thought untouchable.

You are not alone in this work either. And you are needed here.

Chapter 10

Bridging the Divide

Rebuilding Identity, Community, and Faith on New Terms

N o one really prepares you for what comes after. After the rupture. After the unraveling. After you've started to name the harm and tell the truth. A strange space opens up when the system no longer defines you, but nothing else has taken its place. You've walked away, or maybe you've slowly stepped out. You've let go of the roles, rules, and beliefs that used to shape your days. And now. . . it's just quiet.

Not peaceful. Not grounded. Just unfamiliar.

This is the part that often gets missed. The moment when the world goes still, and you're left standing in it without a map. You're not who you were. But you're not quite sure who you are either. There's no clear next step. No new identity waiting. Just space. And maybe that feels like emptiness. Or maybe, underneath the fear, it feels like possibility.

This is where becoming begins.

Not the kind of becoming they talked about in church. Not the becoming that meant selflessness and submission. Not the version of you that needed to prove or perform to be seen. This is different. This is the quiet, steady work of becoming the version of you who has always been there. The one who had to go quiet to survive. The one who learned how to be good, how to be small, how to be whatever was expected.

She didn't disappear. She's still here. And she's starting to stir.

Becoming yourself is not about going back. It's not about returning to who you used to be before the system shaped you. It's about walking into something new, something unknown, something yours. It doesn't come with clarity or confidence, at least not right away. It comes with pausing. Listening. Choosing one small truth at a time. And letting that truth guide you forward.

You don't need to know exactly who you are to begin. You just need to stop pretending to be who they needed you to be. That's where it starts.

And before you let go of her, the version of you who stayed quiet, followed the rules, and did everything right, I want you to pause. She kept you safe. She got you here. She deserves compassion, not shame.

Becoming yourself doesn't mean discarding who you were. It means loving her enough to stop asking her to carry it all.

Unraveled, But Not Broken

When the system unravels, it doesn't just take your beliefs. It takes your roles, your language, your sense of safety. The rhythms that shaped your days. The definitions of what made you good, what made you worthy. It's not just one thing that falls apart; it's everything. And for a while, it can feel like all that's left is what you've lost.

But loss isn't the whole story. And as painful as this unraveling is, it might be the first honest space you've had in years.

This is where the noise begins to quiet. Where the urgency to be good or right starts to loosen. Where the internal panic that told you to hurry up and figure it out begins to settle, even just a little. And in that quiet, something else starts to show up. Something softer. Something that doesn't shout or shame or demand. Your own voice.

Becoming yourself doesn't begin with certainty. It begins with listening. Not to the rules. Not to what you were taught was true. But to your body. Your knowing. The quiet stirrings that say this matters. This hurts. This feels good. This doesn't feel like me. You may not have the words right away. But you don't need them. All you need is the pause. The breath. The permission to notice.

That's where self-trust begins. Not in one big moment but in small ones. When you feel something and choose to believe it. When you say no and don't explain. When you feel anger and let it exist. When you rest because you're tired, not because someone said you earned it. These choices may not look like much from the outside. But they matter. They're how trust begins to take root.

Sometimes, choosing yourself looks like letting the anger come. The anger you swallowed for years. The anger that says, "This wasn't okay." "I deserved better." "I mattered then, even when no one saw it." That anger isn't dangerous. It's honest. It's a part of you. And sometimes, it's what finally gives you the energy to stop performing.

You don't have to have it all figured out to begin. You don't have to be fully healed to be whole. You are not broken. You're becoming. And the more you listen, the more you realize you were never actually lost. You were just never given permission to hear yourself before.

Living With People Who Stay

There will be moments when the ache hits before you even walk in the door. When you feel the tension sitting in your chest. When you already know the room will be full of unspoken expectations. Or silence that says more than words ever could. Sometimes it's easier to stay away. To not show up at all. To avoid the discomfort. And some days, that's the right choice.

But there are other days when you choose to show up anyway. Not to prove anything. Not to perform. Just because you want to. Because you still care. Because you deserve to take up space. And when you do, when you walk in without folding yourself back into the shape they remember, something shifts. You are no longer performing to be palatable. You are showing up whole.

And wholeness has impact.

When you show up as your full self, it disrupts things. Sometimes gently. Sometimes not. It might make the room uncomfortable. People may not know how to respond. They may avoid eye contact. They may try to steer the conversation toward something safer. They may sit in silence or offer you a version of kindness that still holds a hint of grief. Your authenticity will stir something in them. And it might make them uncomfortable.

That doesn't mean you're doing it wrong.

Learning to stay rooted in yourself, even when others don't understand, is part of becoming. It takes time. It takes practice. Some days it will feel strong. Some days it will feel lonely. But you'll begin to notice that you can survive their discomfort. You can hold your own truth without softening it to make other people more comfortable. You can still love them. And you can let them sit with the gap between who you were and who you are becoming.

You don't owe anyone your performance. You don't have to disappear to belong. And you don't have to carry the weight of their disappointment as proof of your love. You can simply be. Fully. Honestly. Present.

And even if no one says it out loud, your presence will tell the truth.

You're not surviving anymore. You're becoming.

Reclaiming Language, Ritual, and Meaning

Leaving the system doesn't mean you stop craving meaning. It doesn't mean you stop needing something sacred. It just means you've stopped letting someone else define what that is.

At first, you might reject all of it. The words. The scriptures. The prayers. The spaces. It makes sense. When something has been used to silence you, control your body, and shape your worth, it's hard to separate what hurt you from what once held you. So you throw it all away for a while. You need the distance. You need to breathe.

But then something soft starts to stir. A question maybe. A memory. A moment that catches your breath. And suddenly, you miss it. Not the rules. Not the system. But the part that made you feel connected. Held. Or grounded.

This is the part where some people feel lost all over again. Because they thought healing meant rejecting everything. But healing is not about rejection. It's about reclamation. It's about choosing what stays. What gets redefined. What gets released.

You might find yourself reaching for a prayer. Not because you believe it the same way but because it connects you to something deeper. You might feel drawn to ritual again, lighting a candle, walking in nature, listening to a song that holds something words can't. These things don't have to be religious to be sacred. They just have to be real.

For some people, spirituality rises again in new ways. Not as obedience. Not as submission. But as presence. Breath. Stillness. A moment that feels wide and quiet and alive. For others, meaning shows up in grief rituals, in movement, in ancestral practices, in the rhythm of making tea or watering plants or watching the sun rise in silence. For some, meaning comes in naming what is gone. For others, in rebuilding something they never had.

You don't have to reclaim anything. You don't have to believe in anything. You don't have to label what you feel. But if something calls to you, gently, curiously, without pressure, you get to listen.

You get to ask, is this mine? Does this feel good in my body? Does this feel like truth?

You don't need to explain it. You don't need to make it align with any system. And you don't need to carry the parts that once felt sacred if they no longer feel safe.

Reclamation is about agency. Not rescuing what was. But allowing space for what's becoming.

Choosing Yourself in Daily Ways

Becoming yourself rarely shows up in big, dramatic moments. Most of the time, it begins in the quiet. The pause. The space between what you used to do and what you're starting to allow. You start saying no when you used to say yes. You pause before agreeing to something that doesn't feel right. You feel your body tense, and you actually notice it, maybe for the first time. And instead of pushing through, you soften. Not because it's easy but because you're learning how to stay with yourself.

These moments don't always look brave on the outside. But they are. They're the kind of bravery that happens mid-conversation, in the middle of a decision, when no one else sees it, but you do. Your body sees it. Your nervous system sees it. And with time, it begins to trust that you won't abandon yourself the way you once did.

Some days, choosing yourself means doing less. Other days, it means doing something new. Wearing the thing. Saying what's true. Leaving the room. These aren't just habits. They're identity work. They're what it means to live in alignment, even when it feels unfamiliar.

And sometimes, it means letting the anger rise. Letting it be there. Letting it say, "That wasn't okay." Letting it remind you that something in you has always known the truth. Anger doesn't mean you're regressing. It means you're no longer swallowing what needed to be said. It means something in you is waking up.

You won't always get it right. You'll still override your gut sometimes. You'll catch yourself slipping back into old patterns. That's okay. That's part of it. Because choosing yourself also means choosing to come back. Again and again. With kindness. With presence. With a little more awareness than you had last time.

Self-trust isn't built through perfection. It's built through returning. One moment at a time. One small act of honesty at a time. It's not just about feeling better. It's about becoming someone your body can trust.

And yes, there will be moments where it feels hard. Where you feel selfish. Where other people don't understand. Where your "no" causes friction. That doesn't mean you're doing it wrong. It means you're doing something different.

The people who benefit from your compliance might not celebrate your growth. But that doesn't make your boundaries wrong. It makes them real.

You are not here to be agreeable. You are here to be whole.

And every time you choose what's true instead of what's expected, you are becoming.

Self-Trust as a Daily Practice

For a long time, trusting yourself wasn't encouraged. It was framed as selfish. Dangerous. Even sinful. You were taught that your feelings couldn't be trusted, that your desires would lead you astray, that your thoughts needed to be filtered through someone else's authority before they were valid. You learned to check yourself at every turn, against a higher power, a leader, a man, a system. Your job was to obey, not to know.

So it makes sense that self-trust still feels unfamiliar. It makes sense that your body braces when you start listening to yourself. Because for years, trust meant doing what was expected. Safety lived in compliance. Worth lived in being agreeable, teachable, and quiet.

Now, you're doing something different.

You're learning to choose you. In the small moments. In the way you pause. In the way you notice. In the way you believe what you feel, even when no one else does. This isn't about reaching some final place of confidence or clarity. It's about learning to come back to yourself. Over and over again.

Because you won't always catch it. You'll still override your knowing sometimes. You'll say yes when you meant no. You'll stay silent when something inside you is screaming. You'll feel the old pattern and follow it out of habit or fear. And when that happens, the work isn't to shame yourself. The work is to return. To notice. To hold yourself gently. And to try again.

That's what self-trust looks like. Not perfection. Not always getting it right. Just presence. Just honesty. Just the willingness to come back after you've left.

It's a practice. A daily one. A rhythm of showing up, listening, choosing, and forgiving. A rhythm of slowly becoming someone you can trust, not because you always get it right but because you keep coming back.

You may feel anger rise in your body: unexpected, sharp, overwhelming. That doesn't mean you're doing it wrong. It means you're finally listening. Anger isn't the opposite of clarity. It's often the path to it.

Self-trust is also learning not to shame the part of you who didn't know better yet. The version of you who stayed quiet. Who did what was expected to stay safe. She wasn't wrong. She wasn't weak. She was surviving. And she deserves tenderness, not judgment.

You don't need permission to trust yourself. You don't need a new spiritual framework. You don't need to replace one belief system with another. You just need to keep listening. Keep returning. Keep choosing your truth, even when it's quiet.

Especially then.

A Soft Return

There's a point in the healing where you stop pushing so hard. You stop scanning for danger in every conversation. You stop preparing your defense before you've even walked into the room. Something shifts, and your body begins to settle. Not because everything is perfect but because you've finally stopped abandoning yourself.

This is the soft return.

Not to the system. Not to the old version of you. But to your body. To your breath. To the part of you that no longer feels the need to earn your place in the world.

It's not a big moment. It doesn't come with clarity or fireworks. Sometimes, it feels like noticing you're laughing and not overthinking it. Or you sit through a holiday and don't completely shut down. You say no and don't apologize. You rest and don't feel guilty. It's not loud, but it's honest. And it means something's different.

This isn't about confidence. It's about ease. It's about being with yourself without performance. It's about letting your nervous system come out of high alert, even for a little while. And when that happens, you realize you're not fighting anymore. You're just living.

And maybe, for the first time, you feel it: this life, this version of you, is being built from the inside out.

You might even feel tenderness for the version of you who couldn't show up like this before. The one who held everything together. The one who made herself small to survive. She deserves that softness. She deserves to be met with love, not criticism. She did the best she could.

You Are Already Becoming

There's no final moment of clarity. No certificate that says you've arrived. Becoming yourself isn't a destination. It's a process. A rhythm. A daily unfolding.

You won't always recognize it while it's happening. Some days you'll feel like you're right back at the beginning. But then, something will shift. You'll notice that you're not shrinking. You'll notice that your no comes more easily. That your yes feels honest. That you're not constantly checking yourself against someone else's expectations.

You'll still have moments of doubt. You'll still feel lonely. Because becoming can be isolating. Sometimes, you'll be the only one in the room choosing truth over comfort. The only one willing to live outside the old rules. But that loneliness doesn't mean you're lost. It means you're no longer living on someone else's terms.

And through it all, you will come back to yourself. Again and again. Not because you've finally figured everything out but because you're learning that you don't have to.

You don't need to be certain to be grounded. You don't need to be fearless to be free. You only need to keep listening. Keep choosing. Keep showing up.

You're already doing it.

You're already becoming.

Epilogue

You Were Always Worthy. Exactly the Way You Are.

You made it here. To the end of the book. But not the end of your story. Not even close.

Maybe you're sitting with more questions than answers. Maybe you're still sorting through rubble or wondering if you're allowed to stop surviving and start living. Maybe you're somewhere in between. All of that belongs here.

There was never going to be a final moment of clarity. No finish line. No perfect version of you waiting on the other side of this work. There's just this: a breath. A pause. A soft recognition that you've already been becoming, even in the moments when you felt like you were unraveling.

And maybe, for the first time, there's also space for choice. Not the kind shaped by fear or obligation. But the kind that comes from listening inward. From hearing your own voice rise, even if it shakes. You don't have to choose the way someone else would. And you don't need to justify the choice you make. There is no right way forward, only your way. You are allowed to choose without shame and judgment because you are the one living your life. And that, in itself, is sacred.

I think of a dear friend of mine. Someone I've walked alongside for years. She spent so long believing she had to earn love by disappearing, by taking care of everyone else around her. But over time, she began to let herself be fully seen. She started offering herself the kind of love she never knew she deserved. And it changed everything. She began to speak her truth without apology. To cry when she needed to. To rest. To take up space. And as she loved herself more fully, her children started loving themselves more tenderly. They began to speak to themselves with softness. With trust. With the kind of language that says, "I am already enough." Because they were watching her learn how to believe it for herself.

I think of a woman I interviewed who stayed in the church, not because she was pretending, but because she found a way to live with integrity inside it. She built a community that truly saw her. She learned to use her voice and ask for what she needed. Her husband listened. Together, they rebuilt something, not on silent suffering, but on mutual respect and honest conversation. She found peace in the space between religious belief and personal spirituality. It wasn't black or white. It was hers.

I think of Hannah and all the women like Hannah I know. The strength it takes to speak. To say it out loud. To name what happened. To stop protecting the people who hurt them. To stop protecting the system that kept them quiet. I think of the way their worlds changed.

In all kinds of ways. Good and bad. Hard and easy. Relationships shifted. Some disappeared. Some grew deeper. Some things broke that couldn't be repaired. And some things began to heal in ways they never thought possible.

Some stayed. Some left. Some found their way back to themselves in unexpected places. And some walked away completely. Most have found a deeper joy because they finally stopped asking for permission to be whole and learned to love themselves fully and stand in their inherent worth and power.

But now, they breathe differently. They speak without shrinking. They say no without shame and yes with joy. They aren't trying to go back to who they were before. They're learning how to stay with themselves. How to tell the truth and love themselves unconditionally. They're building something new. It's still messy. Still unfolding. But it's theirs. And they are still becoming.

And I think of my story. How those core beliefs were so deeply woven into me, I didn't know where they ended and I began. They shaped how I loved. How I stayed small. How I disappeared to stay safe. Every version of myself was built around what I thought I had to be in order to be worthy.

When I finally chose healing, it didn't happen all at once. It came in layers. In softness and anger. In grief and release. In learning to let go of who I thought I needed to be. And slowly, everything began to shift. My life changed. My world changed. My becoming was happening.

And then, there was music. A part of me I thought I had to leave behind. I believed letting it go was proof of my faith. That sacrifice was love. So I buried it. Even though it had always brought me to life.

But healing brought me back to it. Not for performance. Not to prove anything. Just because it was mine. Now, I sit at the piano and play for no reason but joy. I sing because it is fun. I join the local orchestra when I can, and I love every minute of it. I play drums with my kids. It's loud and messy and joyful.

The betrayal I experienced took music from me. I gave it up, thinking that was what God asked of me. But now I know music wasn't what needed to be sacrificed. It was never the problem. It has always been a part of me. And it will be part of my future.

For so long, I judged myself for how I moved through the world. For speaking too freely. For needing too much. For trying too hard. For fawning, overachieving, and staying silent. I thought all of it meant I was broken.

But now, when I look back, I see something else entirely. I see a girl who was doing what she had to do. A girl who was surviving. And I finally, truly believe she makes sense; I make sense.

And one of the gifts I wasn't expecting was that I get to do it differently for my kids. I get to teach them how to truly love themselves. How to care for themselves without apology. I get to love them in a way that helps them love themselves unconditionally. I get to show them how to use their voice. How to stand up for themselves. How to live in a body they love and are proud of. How to understand their brain and their emotions and how to get their needs met with clarity and confidence. I get to give them what I never had. And that changes everything.

You don't have to be fully healed to be worthy of love. You don't have to be sure of everything to take the next step. You don't have to perform a perfect life to belong to yourself.

Every change you make creates ripples. You may never see how far they reach, but they matter. You don't know how those ripples will impact the people around you. But they will. Keep going. Keep becoming.

You were always worthy. Exactly the way you are.

And I hope, more than anything, that you never forget that again.

www.ingramcontent.com/pod-product-compliance
Lightning Source LLC
Chambersburg PA
CBHW031122020426
42333CB00012B/192